Dear Reader:

The book you are about to ~~read~~ is ~~part of the~~
St. Martin's True Crime Lib~~rary that Publishers Weekly~~
calls "the leader in true crim~~e...month,~~ we offer you a fascinating account of the latest, most sensational crime that has captured the national attention. St. Martin's is the publisher of Tina
Dirmann's VANISHED AT SEA, the story of a former child actor who
posed as a yacht buyer in order to lure an older couple out to sea,
then robbed them and threw them overboard to their deaths. John
Glatt's riveting and horrifying SECRETS IN THE CELLAR shines a
light on the man who shocked the world when it was revealed that
he had kept his daughter locked in his hidden basement for 24
years. In the Edgar-nominated WRITTEN IN BLOOD, Diane Fanning
looks at Michael Petersen, a Marine-turned-novelist found guilty
of beating his wife to death and pushing her down the stairs of
their home—only to reveal another similar death from his past.
In the book you now hold, A PROFESSOR'S RAGE, Michele McPhee
unlocks the secrets of a particularly dramatic cold case.

St. Martin's True Crime Library gives you the stories behind the
headlines. Our authors take you right to the scene of the crime and
into the minds of the most notorious murderers to show you what
really makes them tick. St. Martin's True Crime Library paperbacks are better than the most terrifying thriller, because it's all
true! The next time you want a crackling good read, make sure it's
got the St. Martin's True Crime Library logo on the spine—you'll
be up all night!

Charles E. Spicer, Jr.
Executive Editor, St. Martin's True Crime Library

A PROFESSOR'S RAGE

The Chilling True Story of Harvard Ph.D. Amy Bishop,

Her Brother's Mysterious Death,

and the Shooting Spree That Shocked the Nation

Michele R. McPhee

St. Martin's Paperbacks

A PROFESSOR'S RAGE

Copyright © 2011 by Michele R. McPhee.

For information address St. Martin's Press, 175 Fifth Avenue, New York, NY 10010.

EAN: 978-0-312-53529-2

Printed in the United States of America

St. Martin's Paperbacks edition / July 2011

St. Martin's Paperbacks are published by St. Martin's Press, 175 Fifth Avenue, New York, NY 10010.

10 9 8 7 6 5 4 3 2 1

For my mother, Sheila Patricia Seward McPhee

ACKNOWLEDGMENTS

There are so many people who are deserving of thanks who cannot be named on these pages. They know who they are, and that their efforts to make this an accurate record of a shooting that took place so long ago are appreciated.

Some will call this a book of police corruption. I want to note that there were police officers who battled to investigate fully the circumstances of Seth Bishop's death. Massachusetts enjoys a long and infamous reputation as a state steeped in political buffoonery and incompetence when it comes to public safety. I will leave it at that.

Thanks also to great diplomats to the media like David Traub of the Norfolk County District Attorney's Office. Also, police chiefs are inundated with minutiae, so I am grateful to Paul Frazier of Braintree and Paul Nikas for putting up with my requests for public records.

I would like to thank my agent, Jane Dystel, and my editor, Allison Strobel. And of course I want to thank Charlie Spicer for counting me among his true crime writers.

On a personal note, this book would not have been possible without the prodding and coddling that came from a great writer and a good friend, Joe Keohane.

ACKNOWLEDGMENTS

My sister Erin Donovan shows up at every book event—thank you, along with my godparents Joan and Dick Dennis. My parents, Bruce and Sheila McPhee, and my sister Shannon have always been supportive.

And thanks to MPH.

A PROFESSOR'S RAGE

1

Tom Pettigrew wiped a dirty hand on his blue mechanic's pants and glanced around an auto body bay at Dave Dinger Ford—a garage owned by a buddy of his in the working class suburb of Braintree, Massachusetts. It was December 6, 1986, and Pettigrew was jumpy, looking around, waiting for some unwelcome visitor or other to turn up. He'd been that way since he stole $25,000 from an ATM two weeks earlier. He had moved the cash around a bit until it was stashed in his toolbox at the shop.

Pettigrew was a punk twenty-year-old Irish-American guy from the South Shore of Boston. He was a good-looking, personable kid who lived with his mom and held down two jobs, but he had a knack for getting himself into trouble. He was always on the hunt for a big score. Where others saw danger, he saw opportunity.

It was kind of like a brand growing up Irish on the South Shore in those days. People like to say that Boston is segregated mainly by race, but that's not true. It's segregated first and foremost by geography. Back then, every neighborhood in Boston, and every town around it, had its own look, even its own distinct accent. Pettigrew could clearly be picked out of a lineup as a South Shore guy. He sported shell-toed Adidas sneakers. His blond, curly hair was left alone, not shaved on the side like the North Shore guys' hair. South Shore guys abhorred muscle shirts, or "wife beaters," and wore pastel-colored, collared Izod shirts to dress up and rock band shirts for their downtime. Pettigrew was into metal—the music that in the late 1980s had brought people from the North Shore and the South Shore together—so he was often seen wearing T-shirts from concerts he had attended at the Centrum in Worcester: Quiet Riot, maybe, or Black Sabbath. Instead of the North Shore's gold chains, guys from the South Shore wore Irish Claddagh rings upside down with the heart facing out to signal to women that they were single (even if they weren't). When the North Shore and South Shore guys came together, brawls often erupted as the conspicuously dressed factions fought to properly represent their respective home turfs. Pettigrew was one of those punks, a hood rat who knew how to use his fists. Sometimes he would throw the first punch just to remind his friends of that very fact.

On that cold Saturday afternoon, December 6, 1986, Tom Pettigrew didn't need to throw any punches to assure his friends of his manhood. They were awed by him. He had practically robbed a bank. He stood inside the auto body shop, glancing around. Then he called his two buddies, Dino Malchionno and Johnny Sullivan. He needed to calm down. And there was only one way to settle that anxiety. Pettigrew pulled a fat joint from the pocket of his grease-stained pants and then leaned on the trunk of his black 1986 Thunderbird Coupe five-speed, shining in the repair bay. His baby. It was in perfect condition, with a black-on-black interior. Now that Tom had a new revenue source he was going to add some speed features that would make him unbeatable in a drag race. There was always a possibility for a drag race in a city like Braintree. He leaned in the window, popped in the cigarette lighter, and pushed the head of the joint into the orange glow. He sucked in a deep hit while Dino and Johnny, recently arrived, stood and waited.

"Boys. You ready to count the take?" Pettigrew asked as he took a long toke. He bulged out his eyes as he held his breath, his cheeks puffed out. He exhaled, looked at the grease under his nails, and scrubbed his palms against the rough cotton fabric of his mechanic's pants again. There was something about crisp, new $100 bills that made him want clean hands. Sure, he could have counted the cash alone. But the robbery was not just about the money. It was about the moxie. And Tom Pettigrew wanted everyone in his crew to remember he had it.

"Let's see what we have here."

He didn't have to ask twice. Time had slowed to an agonizing crawl since Pettigrew had come to Dino's house all sweaty and guilty looking on the dawn side of midnight a few days earlier, with a lumpy duffel bag he wanted to stash there. Dino had let him, though he and Johnny Sullivan wondered whether Pettigrew's talk of the score was nothing more than braggadocio, or maybe even drug-induced wishful thinking. Dino was tempted to look in the bag, sure. He had hung around with Tom Pettigrew long enough to know that the guy was capable of almost anything—especially with a few drinks in him. But Dino decided to leave well enough alone, lest his fingerprints become the only evidence on a bag from a crime scene. That morning, Pettigrew had come back for the bag. He took it to the garage and transferred its contents to his Diehard Toolbox. Dino and Johnny had been on pins and needles for days. It was killing them. And it was finally time to find out what was in the bag.

Pettigrew grinned as he opened the box. Hidden under tools were bundles of $100 and $20 bills. His lifelong buddies gasped. "Holy shit," Dino said. The cash in the toolbox seemed limitless. Slowly, Pettigrew spread piles of $1,000 stacks across the trunk of the Thunderbird, which was painted a black so shiny that the fresh new bills against the sports car looked as green as fake grass. The take was $25,000: more money than any of them had seen in their lives. With the money spread out on the car's trunk, Pettigrew took another hit off the joint and told them how he had done it.

Pettigrew worked the 4 p.m.-to-midnight shift as a clerk at the Convenient Food Mart, a little store right up on Washington Street, not far from the auto body shop. It was a convenient location because he could work at the body shop all day and then walk over to the store for the night shift. Better still, when an armored car came by once a week to refill the store's ATM, it was during Pettigrew's shift.

"I was working the night shift," he told his buddies. "No one was around. I was sweeping up the back near the ATM machine. The thing had a safe like on the back and every night I would just get this feeling to pull on the safe handle to see if it would open. I would yell out to the kid that I was working with—John Bradley—'Pick a number' and try the safe. It never worked.

"But that night the door didn't close all the way. I was like, 'Holy shit, the door's open.' I could see the money cassettes all lined up."

Pettigrew had pulled a pair of gloves off the deli counter and put them on. He kept his eyes on the mirror positioned over the door so he could spot any new customers—potential rats—coming in the store. Then he started to pull the cassettes out of the safe. His neck tensed as he wondered if there would be some sort of alarm to alert the armored truck guards that the money had been tampered with. He stacked the cassettes near the safe just in case and waited. It seemed like hours, but after forty-five minutes it was clear no one was coming back.

"I didn't even know how much money was in them," Pettigrew said. Then for effect, he sucked in another hit off the joint. "I ran out to my car and grabbed my gym bag and just started filling it up."

Of course every convenience store had a video camera, so Pettigrew and Bradley erased it. Those things always malfunctioned anyway. They grabbed Windex from behind the deli counter and wiped down the inside and the outside of the safe. Then they stuffed the money in a bag.

"It was fucking awesome. No one even noticed," Pettigrew bragged.

Once their shift at the Food Mart ended, Pettigrew suggested he and Bradley count the take at Bradley's place. Bradley, no seasoned crook, was terrified, but he agreed anyway. The charismatic Pettigrew could be hard to resist. Just as the pair had pulled all the money out of the cassettes from the ATM, however, Bradley's older brother came home. That surprise cost Pettigrew five grand. He and Bradley peeled off half of one bundle and handed it to Bradley's brother in exchange for his silence, or so Pettigrew said. Pettigrew stuffed the rest of the money back into the duffel bag and dropped it at Dino's place with a promise that the bounty would be spread around.

The morning after the heist, Braintree police detectives had shown up to fingerprint the ATM. Pettigrew wasn't worried. He had carefully wiped down every surface. He had worn the deli gloves. Of course, Pettigrew and his coworker were the prime suspects in the case. The Braintree police were so sure that they were involved—especially after they discovered that the night shift security videotape had been mysteriously erased—that they called in the FBI to give both men lie detector tests. Then again, the money had been FDIC-insured, so the feds would have been called in even if the cops didn't immediately suspect the two hood rats working the night shift. Now they just had to prove it. So far they had not. Somehow, Pettigrew beat the lie detector test. Surprisingly, so did Bradley. The cops had nothing.

With the FBI lie detector test behind him and the detectives off his tail, Pettigrew finally felt comfortable enough to tally the score. He'd transferred the loot from his bag to his toolbox in preparation for the big unveiling at the garage. He knew it was a major score. He had seen the armored car drivers fill the machine enough times to know how fully they stocked it. Now it was almost a high to count the cash. It seemed appropriate to do it on a sexy machine like the five-speed T-Bird. Made him feel like a high roller. A big shot.

Pettigrew, Dino, and Johnny "Sully" Sullivan high-fived one another as the count was confirmed. A thousand dollars in each bundle. Twenty bundles, plus the half-stack left over after he'd tossed his coworker's brother five grand to shut him up. Nice. Big money for small-time punks in the late '80s. Ecstatic but still uneasy, the boys began to talk about the likelihood that the bills were marked and accounted for. The discussion turned to ideas: schemes to spend the bills undetected, or sell them at a loss to launder them. Marked stolen bills all spent in Braintree might be just the thing the cops needed to pin the heist on them.

Suddenly, there was a loud banging from the back door of the shop leading to the rear stairwell. It was roughly 2:30 in the afternoon, and ordinarily no one entered the auto body shop from back there. "What the fuck?" Dino said. "You hear that?" Johnny Sullivan began to shovel the bundles of cash back into the tool-box as Pettigrew moved toward the back. The body shop was part of the Dinger Ford dealership, and an employee there, Jeff Doyle, had also heard the noise and had begun to make his way toward the commotion. The way the dealership was set up was that Dinger Ford sold cars in the back and there were three bays that private mechanics could rent out to conduct their own side business—like the auto shop. It was a cold Satur-day. Tom Pettigrew and his buddies were the only ones working in the bays and Jeff Doyle was trying to un-load Fords off the lot for the dealership. Both men heard a clatter near the back entrance that linked the dealer-ship to the repair bays.

Pettigrew swung open a door and stopped short. His chest bumped right into the business end of a Mossberg 500A pump-action shotgun. Aiming it at him was a young woman with sharp-cut bangs. The gun actually thumped him hard enough to leave a bruise. Jeff Doyle stood next to him without saying a word. "Whoa," Pet-tigrew said. He began to sweat. For a minute he thought it was a holdup. *How the hell did this girl know about the money? Who is this bitch?*

Despite the frigid New England temperatures, the tall, heavyset woman was wearing a heavy blue jacket over her grey sweatpants and white sneakers without socks. She was also surprisingly calm for a twenty-one-year-old who had just shot her own brother. His body lay unmov-ing on the kitchen floor of her family's picturesque New England Victorian home just around the corner from the car dealership. There were no tears. Her eyes were fixed on the men in front of her. A lock of hair was blown into her eyes, but she made no move to brush it away. She held the shotgun steady. Her name was Amy Bishop, and she would become very famous about two and a half decades from that day.

"Put your hands up," she ordered. "I said put your hands up!"

Pettigrew's tattooed arms shot straight up into the air. Doyle followed his lead.

"I need a car," Bishop said. She was nervously looking around but her grip was steadfast on the weapon. "Give me your keys."

Pettigrew thought to himself: *What about the money?* Truth is, Pettigrew was a street guy. While it was wholly unlikely that he would give up the cash, there was absolutely no way in hell he was giving this crazy bitch his Thunderbird.

"I just got in a fight with my husband," she stammered. "He's trying to hurt me. I have to get out of here. He's going to kill me. You have to give me a car. He's looking for me."

Pettigrew looked over at Jeff Doyle. Pettigrew had grown up in Quincy, a hardscrabble blue-collar town on the southern border of Boston. Doyle lived in Marshfield, which was considered a wealthy waterfront community. Pettigrew knew the guy, but they weren't friends. Their backgrounds were too different. At that moment they shared something in common, though: the will to stay alive.

"Step back," the woman barked, keeping the gun trained on them the entire time.

Both men stared at one another as if the look could form a plan. They nodded. Then they ran like hell for cover.

"I remember running with my hands up," Petti-grew would say more than two decades after his encounter with Amy Bishop. He ran out of the garage, down Washington Street, and flagged down a passing patrol car—an atypical move for a guy like Tom Pettigrew, especially considering he had in his possession a tool-box stuffed with stolen cash—but police had already been called to the scene. Bishop had attempted to car-jack a driver before she ran into Pettigrew, but the would-be victim took off, raced to her nearby home, just down the street from the Bishops on Hollis Avenue, and called 911.

Chaos ensued. Police radios began to squawk orders to the patrol cops working the city. It was 2:22 p.m. Braintree police officers hurtled toward the scene when another call came in. This one was from Judy Bishop, Amy's mother, who said in a surprisingly calm voice: "My daughter just shot my son." It could have been the shock, but the mother's voice did not quiver. The 911 operator thought it might be a prank call. It wasn't.

As commanding officers sped to the Bishop home at 46 Hollis Avenue, patrol officers began to hunt for the woman with the gun. After Pettigrew and Doyle got away, Bishop had made her way toward another nearby business called Village News, a newspaper distribution center. Workers, primarily a cluster of teenagers who loaded bundles of local newspapers—the *Boston Globe,* the *Boston Herald*, and the *Patriot Ledger*—onto wait-ing trucks, looked up at the sound of approaching sirens. Amy Bishop was weaving through parked cars. The shotgun was cradled against her chest like a baby. She looked dazed.

"What the fuck?" Tim Greene, who was 17, mumbled aloud to himself. "Guys, check this out. There is some girl out here with a gun!"

Greene turned around and Bishop now had the gun pointed directly at him.

"Do you have a car?" the woman asked.

"No." Panicked, Greene yelled inside: "Hey, this girl needs a car."

"No fucking way," came the response from inside the building where Greene's coworkers crouched behind stacks of newspapers. A *Globe* truck pulled into the lot. So did Braintree police cruisers. Greene and his coworkers shouted over the din of the police radios toward the cops.

"She's right there! She has a gun!"

Braintree Police Officer Ron Solimini was the first to spot Amy Bishop out of the corner of his eye making her way toward the trucks. He picked up his radio and transmitted a message: "I have located the suspect in the rear of Village News on Washington and Parkingway Drive." He swung his cruiser around.

Solimini climbed out of his cruiser and began to make his way toward her with his gun drawn at his side, clutched in his right hand next to his holster. As he approached the woman, she just stared at him wild-eyed and refused to lower the weapon.

"Miss Bishop seemed frightened, disoriented, and confused," Solimini told his bosses. "She kept both her hands on the shotgun at all times as I was talking to her trying to get her to drop the gun." He moved toward her with the gun steady at his side. "Drop it!" he ordered. The woman just stared. He softened his tone. "Look, hon. Why don't you put that down and come with me over to the cruiser? We can straighten this all out."

Then another Braintree police officer arrived. Timmy Murphy moved slowly from the other side of the building so the woman wouldn't see him. Solimini spotted his fellow officer and tried to keep Amy Bishop's eyes on him. Murphy jumped up on the back of the news truck and tried to see which would be the most successful way to grab the powerful shotgun from her without it going off. He knew it would take five pounds of pressure to squeeze off a shell. He leaped from the back of the truck, got about five feet behind the woman, and pulled out his own gun. He pointed it at the back of her head.

"Drop it!"

Nothing. Bishop didn't move.

"Drop it!"

Again. She acted as if she didn't hear him.

By then other cops had arrived on the scene. Greene remembers one officer screeched with his hands shaking: "Put that gun down or I am going to blow your fucking head off." Those types of commands usually don't find their way into a police report.

After a third and final command, Murphy moved in behind her and grabbed the end of the shotgun. She loosened her grip and the weapon fell to the concrete with a clank. Murphy grabbed the gun as Solimini held the woman's wrists. The gunpoint standoff lasted roughly ninety seconds, but for the suburban cops unaccustomed to that kind of action, it seemed a lot longer.

The weapon was loaded. Murphy patted the woman down and felt another shell in her pocket. What Murphy didn't know was that the shotgun had been fired twice already that morning—meaning the woman had already racked and re-racked the weapon within the hour of her arrest.

Amy Bishop was not after Tom Pettigrew's ill-gotten money. She wasn't trying to escape an abusive husband. Amy Bishop was on the run. She had blasted a hole through her little brother's chest in her family's kitchen around the corner from Village News. Even as

Seth Bishop bled to death face down on the linoleum floor, his horrified mother was seeking to deal with the fallout from the shells squeezed off by her daughter that just blew up her family. And Judy Bishop had enough juice in the town to help her. Attractive, blonde, and powerful in local politics, Judy served on the town committee, an elected legislative panel of 240 people who had control over how the town spent its money, including how much money was funneled to the police department. She was close to Police Chief John Polio. She put a call in to her friend before the ambulance even arrived to pick up her son.

At 2:45 p.m., Officer Solimini transported Amy to the Braintree Police Station in handcuffs. As they drove the less than two miles to the station, Amy had an eerie look on her face. Without a tremor in her voice she volunteered: "I had an argument with my father." Solimini did not ask her to elaborate. He wanted to get her into a booking room. This was a big case and he wanted to handle it by the rules. Besides, he was still rattled at how close he had come to potentially being hit by a shotgun blast. He would write up his encounter with Amy Bishop and his experience with her in the booking room.

Solimini recited her Miranda rights. "Do you want to talk to me, Amy," he asked. "Did anything happen at home? Everything all right?"

Solimini recounted the conversation in a police report that he filled out that night, writing:

> *She stated that earlier there had been a family "spat" and that she had gone to her room. (Unknown at this time how much earlier this family "spat" had been.) She stated that she loaded the shotgun because she had been worried about "robbers" coming into the house. Sometime in the past her brother had shown her how to*

*load the shotgun but not how to unload it. After load-
ing the shotgun, she accidentally fired a round in her
bedroom which struck a lamp and the wall. She tried to
cover this up so her mother would not see the damage.
Sometime later (again how much later is unknown
at this time) she went downstairs and into the kitchen
where she approached her mother and asked her if she
knew how to unload the shotgun she was carrying. She
said her mother told her not to point it at anyone. At
this point she turned and the shotgun went off striking
her brother. I asked her if she shot her brother on purpose and she said no. At this point her mother came
into the booking room with Sgt. [Kenneth] Brady and
[her] mother said she didn't want to make any further
statements or be asked any more questions. Amy then
said she wouldn't answer any more questions. I left the
booking area.*

Many Braintree cops would soon be outraged to learn
that Amy Bishop was not charged. Not with a single
crime. The commanding officer on shift that afternoon
was a well-respected guy named Pete D'Amico. The
captain in charge of detectives, Theodore Buker, would
be called in from home. This had the potential to be
problematic, so the brass needed to be involved.

Buker would be the one to declare that "no charges
would be brought against Amy Bishop at this time."
The Northeastern University student wouldn't spend
even an hour behind bars. Not for killing her brother.
Not for the attempted carjacking of a neighbor. Not for
threatening Tom Pettigrew and Jeff Doyle. Not for bran-
dishing the gun at teenager Tim Greene. Not for refusing
to obey a police command.

Amy Bishop was ordered to be released by the
Braintree Police Chief, John Polio. Literally. He called

the station and ordered that the college student be released into her mother's custody, a decision that would not sit well with the Braintree police officers who had been menaced with the loaded shotgun. Amy would not lay her head on the hard metal of a prison cot on that night in 1986. She would not be fingerprinted or photographed. In fact, no detective would even have an opportunity to fully interrogate her. The case was squashed. She escaped any criminal penalties for that December day. Vague reports would be written by a respected state police trooper assigned to the Norfolk District Attorney's Office. He would later argue he was never armed with real facts about the events of December 6, 1986. Even the initial Braintree police reports were hand-scrawled under the heading: "*accidental shooting.*" That determination had been made official before an investigation could take place.

Judy Bishop was heard telling a police officer that afternoon: "I just lost one child; I am not going to lose both."

Judy Bishop was right . . . for the time being. There would be no jail for her twenty-one-year-old daughter.

Not until the year 2010, when the respected Harvard University–schooled scientist would go on a shooting rampage at the University of Alabama that killed three of her colleagues and left three others wounded.

2

Judy Bishop was waiting by the door when police arrived at the blue Victorian home where she and her husband, Samuel, a Northeastern University professor, had lived with their children. The couple had been together since their college days at the University of Iowa. They were both educated hippies and proud of it. In fact, the couple was well known for being stoic in public. Today was no different. There were no tears rolling down Judy's face. A strange calm had settled over her. Tall and voluptuous with blonde curls that hung naturally to the small of her back, she was a woman of action. She got things done. Her son was facedown on the linoleum floor of her kitchen with a hole ripped through the right side of his chest. Her daughter had run out with the weapon. Her husband hadn't returned from the mall. So the crisis was all on her. She made her way to the door when she heard the sirens.

Hollis Avenue was a leafy, winding street a short walking distance to Braintree Square, a desirable location in the town of roughly 33,000 residents. Braintree, Massachusetts, is a historic place. John Adams—the nation's second president—and his son, John Quincy Adams, who would become the sixth President of the United States, were both born in Old Braintree. The statesman John Hancock and the man who helped Alexander Graham Bell invent the telephone (even if he is rarely credited for it), Thomas A. Watson, were also residents of Braintree. The town was incorporated in 1640 and has always been a well-off enclave, much like its namesake, the English town of Braintree. In the 1980s it had remained upper middle class, desirable for, among other things, its well-maintained public parks system. It was in those parks and in that small town that Seth and Amy Bishop had grown up under the watchful eyes of their parents. Sam was an associate arts professor at Northeastern University who specialized in documentary filmmaking. He looked the part. He was bespectacled with scraggly hair and had a way of studying people intently, as if he wanted to decipher the meaning of each sentence uttered to dissect its layers of meaning. His students loved him. In fact, Hollywood producer David Bushell, whose film credits include the Academy Award winner *Sling Blade*, *Eternal Sunshine of the Spotless Mind*, *Deception*, and *Get Him to the Greek*, credited Sam Bishop in an Oscar speech with providing him the encouragement to move to Los Angeles and pursue a movie career.

Judy Bishop was a somewhat heavyset woman, but she carried her weight with a confidence that made her attractive to the men who served alongside her on the powerful town committee. She knew the high-ranking police officers who ran Braintree and was friendly with the police chief, John Polio. According to police who knew them, both were hard to get along with. Neither cared that they were not well liked in the town. In fact, Judy Bishop was known as a woman who could be sweet and grateful—if she got her way. Polio was wildly unpopular with the rank-and-file police officers. And that was fine with him. While most police chiefs in small towns balanced their power with personality, helping officers get the time off they needed or the cash flow that came with overtime and police details, Polio was about keeping cops in line. Among the brethren, he was famous for compiling what they called "Polio files," which were exactly that: compiled notes about minor mistakes made by the rank and file. In a 1984 interview with the *Patriot Ledger* he told a reporter:

> *You have to understand. I have not had an easy life. I have survived a lot of pain, and I have fought to retain my ideals despite the ugliness and savagery you inevitably run into in this business. So when the attacks get personal, that's when you have to pull away into yourself. Difficult as it is, much as you are hurting and bleeding inside, you have to do that because you are responsible for your actions. Rational detachment doesn't stop the hurt or the bleeding, but I find that it helps. I think of the animal that has been hurt or wounded. He looks for that safe ground; he looks to detach himself from his enemies. And so he finds himself that little knoll, hummock or hay mound to burrow himself into, and he looks for a little solace, a little comfort, a little peace. Well, I don't liken the animal to the man, but it's not unlike that sort of feeling. You can detach to a degree that's almost dangerous, and when I was younger I would sometimes lash out. But now, when I feel the pain festering inside, I know that I have to retreat in order to let it out in a positive way.*

Polio never elaborated on the pain that he suffered. Everyone in town knew that Polio was the youngest of four children whose parents immigrated to the United States from Sicily. When he was three years old, his father died, leaving his mother to raise the kids alone,

supporting the family by working long hours in garment factories. Polio's older brothers were overachievers, and he felt unworthy after both served their countries
with combat careers during World War II while he performed menial jobs as a farmer, an iceman, an apprentice machinist, and a garment worker like his mother, he
told the *Patriot Ledger* reporter. Eventually he entered
the United States Navy and became a sharpshooter. Then
he followed a path that many high school dropouts and
military veterans had taken before him: He became a
cop. Then, at forty, he became Braintree's youngest-ever
police chief in 1962. And like many men who were once
bullied only to become powerful, he used his newly
established cache to ruin other men. He fired them for
having tattoos. He locked up drunk politicians, which
was a huge stain on one's record in a state like Massachusetts where corrupt solons had always enjoyed being
above the law. He even tried to keep track of his officers
by painting patrol cars loud shades of pink and orange
so he could better track their whereabouts. The stunt
made the town the laughingstock of law enforcement
agencies throughout the Commonwealth and earned
Polio the nickname "Rainbow Chief."

"Polio was an absolute nut. Cuckoo. Cuckoo," retired Boston Police Detective Jack Parlon, a former
union official for the BPD, would later say.

Polio didn't care what his brethren in blue said about
him. He made no secret about the fact that he grew up
friendless and that stuck with him throughout his adult
life. He attracted enemies. Some say he even courted
them. "I always felt myself to be inadequate and quite
low on the aptitude scale next to my brothers. I quit
school just to set myself apart from them. It was a way
of saying: 'Notice me too.' But I was really a loser in
my own eyes. I felt cut all the time, socially just cut.

Some who shared my life path might end up citing it as the reason they ended up in Walpole [state prison]. But not me," he told the *Patriot Ledger*.

His friend Judy would come to know the pain that John Polio described as "festering" inside him. Her daughter, Amy, also seemed to have a lot in common with her mom's friend, the police chief. Like Polio, she, too, felt inadequate. Amy had a difficult time making friends and felt that she had to jump up and down and outperform to get her parents' attention. Seth, however, was a different story. Everything came easily for Seth. He was a virtuoso violinist. He was an A student who excelled in math and science. Old ladies loved him. So did his classmates. He wasn't exactly good-looking. Nor was he a standout with the girls, primarily because he was painfully shy. Still, Seth managed to maintain a collection of loyal buddies and earned the respect of school officials. Amy was always the ugly duckling, the outsider who had to work twice as hard as her brother for everything. When she picked out metallic silvery wallpaper for her bedroom with giant pink and purple flowers emblazoned onto it, her mother sighed. "You're going to think this is ugly before long." Judy also berated Amy for cutting her own hair. Judy's hair was naturally gorgeous, lush and blonde with curls that framed her face. Her daughter would take a pair of scissors in the bathroom, cut her bangs short across her forehead; she wore her hair bobbed around the back, sometimes straight, sometimes curly—a hairstyle that would follow her into adulthood. Seth would always tell her that it was cool, that she sported a musician's hairdo that gave her some moxie. It was his nature to assuage his sister's hair-trigger temper with kind words. It had worked throughout their childhoods.

Seth Bishop was probably the only person who knew

how to deal with Amy. In fact, he had a politician's knack for reading people, which was not surprising given his lifelong fascination with the history of his town. He was so obsessed with colonial agitators like John Adams and his younger cousin Sam Adams that he decorated his room with Revolutionary War–themed wallpaper. Even as a little boy he would blurt to his parents' dinner guests, "Did you know John Adams helped draft the Declaration of Independence? Right here? In Braintree?" Just like his hero, John Adams, Seth wanted to attend Harvard University, become an attorney, and fight for the rights of everyone, even the low and loathed.

By this point in his life, Seth Bishop was used to a good scrap. Sure, he tried to squelch Amy's rages. Yet he fought continuously with his older sister. The feud went deeper than typical sibling territoriality. Amy had always resented how easily Seth got along with people. When they were at Braintree High School together, she was the weird girl a year ahead of her little brother. When she graduated in 1983, her yearbook listed her extracurricular activities: "Amy Bishop. National Honor Society 4, Orchestra 1, 2, 3, 4. BHSSA 2, 3. New England Conservatory of Music, Greater Boston Youth Symphony Orchestra. BHS Chamber Orchestra." This was followed by a quote from Lewis Carroll: *"The time has come," the Walrus said, "to talk of many things. Of shoes—and ships—and sealing wax—of cabbages—and kings—And why the sea is boiling hot—and whether pigs have wings."*

And after the strange *Alice in Wonderland* quote, Amy wrote a note for her younger brother: Amy Bishop, I hereby bequeath my violin and music to my brother Seth.

A year later, Seth enrolled at Northeastern, where his father worked, and began to bloom. He made friends easily and got along with his classmates, many of whom were wealthy and hailed from all four corners of the world. Moreover, Seth was a gifted violinist. It was that talent—shown even when he was a small child—that sparked much of the jealousy many saw festering within Amy. Amy would complain that her parents had always favored Seth. She resented him for sucking up to them, for the way he shoveled the snow without having been asked, for how he was always helping old ladies struggling with the groceries. He was the golden child. No matter how much Amy accomplished in science, her brother did better. She was a beautiful violinist, but her brother was a member of the Boston Youth Symphony Orchestra just like his older sister and was named the Braintree High School concertmaster. He won the national high school math award and first prize in the science award in the categories of both chemistry and biology. Even his short stories were good enough to be published in the high school literary magazine, *Stone Soup*.

Even when they were very little, Amy, who was always somewhat homely and had a lazy left eye, may have felt that as long as her brother was around she'd remain largely overlooked. Judy had gone so far as to nickname her son "Dandelion," because his golden locks were so fine they were like petals. He was a gentle boy, she would say. "I remember one day when he was five he came home sobbing," Judy once told the *Braintree Forum & Observer*. "He had a small stain on his new hand-knit blue sweater. He had crushed a robin's egg in his hand by mistake and thought he had killed a baby bird. It took an hour to calm him down," Judy said. "I said to myself, 'How can I send this gentle little boy out into the world.'" She would do so reluctantly. But Seth, her pride and joy, was up to the challenge.

He had already begun to excel at Northeastern University, while his sister, who had already been a student for a full two years when her brother arrived on campus, struggled socially. It didn't help that her boyfriend, Jim Anderson, was also a geek. She had met him at the Dungeons & Dragons club at Northeastern University. Both were biology students. Both were social outcasts. Both had developed reputations as weirdos for being heavily into the fantasy of LARP (Live Action Role-Playing) that the game was famous for. (It was also controversial and had been banned from many prisons because of what some viewed as its demonic and violent elements.)

What made matters worse was that Amy's boyfriend was also viewed as a redneck by his classmates, most of whom hailed from the northeast. He had grown up in Alabama, but his family had moved to the south shore of Massachusetts for his father's job when he was a teenager. He spent his teen years with his family in the town of Foxborough, Massachusetts. He still had that heavy southern accent, thick as corn syrup. The drawl was one of the things Amy Bishop liked about her boyfriend. Even when he was in costume in the Dungeons & Dragons club, she could spot his beer-bulging belly and listened for his drawl. "I knew I loved that woman the minute I laid eyes on her," Anderson would say. "And I knew she felt the same way about me. It was destined."

Seth Bishop and Jimmy Anderson did not pal around. Seth wanted nothing to do with a club full of outcasts and freaks, especially in a college setting. He had already suffered through an awkward phase in high school and didn't want to repeat those lonely school days. He warned Amy that it would be tough for her to make friends outside of the Dungeons & Dragons scene. She didn't listen. Seth always had things come easily to him. He didn't know what it was like to have trouble making friends. This had been going on Amy's entire life.

When Seth bought himself a fire engine–red Camaro, his popularity escalated. The accolades he acquired in high school—the Arion music award; the national high school math award—continued to college. He came in first in every academic challenge, taking first place in the school science fair and then second prize in the Eastern Massachusetts science fair and third in the statewide contest. He didn't even tell his mother about the awards. Over breakfast Judy would shake the newspaper at Amy and muse, "Your brother did it again. Look at him," while pointing at Seth's name in the blurry newsprint. While Amy was chunky, Seth was lean and athletic. Where she was awkward, he was graceful. He could do no wrong.

It was just a few weeks before Christmas. Seth didn't want anything under the tree, he kept telling his parents. They smiled at him. So sweet, this kid. So generous. Amy saw the way her parents looked at him so approvingly. It was hard not to notice.

Was Amy Bishop growing tired of competing with him? On the afternoon of Saturday, December 6, 1986, did she decide to do something about it?

3

Braintree Police sergeant Kenneth Brady was surprised to see Judy Bishop on the front porch when he arrived at 46 Hollis Avenue. A patrol car had arrived before him, and two of his cops, Rick Jordan and Timmy Murphy, were already in the kitchen desperately trying to keep Seth Bishop alive. The officers had found the teen lying on his left side in a mess of blood. The cops quickly turned him over onto his back to try to create an airway. By then the blood had pooled out beneath him like a macabre throw rug. There was a gaping hole in his chest that leaked air in an awful screech. All three cops on the scene were grateful to hear the caterwauling siren from the approaching paramedics team. It was very unlikely the kid was going to survive and the cops did not want to watch him die in front of them. Blood had steeped across the tile floor in the ramshackle kitchen. The cops were grateful when the paramedics showed up to take over.

Sergeant Brady gave the paramedics a nod as they hustled past the strangely silent mom on the porch of the blue Victorian and Brady knew her and into the kitchen. Judy Bishop did not follow them into the kitchen to be with her son. Instead she looked at the police sergeant standing on her porch. She knew Kenneth Brady and

Brady knew her. She was an elected official and every cop in town knew that she had juice when it came to the Braintree Police operating budget. She usually sided with police over tightfisted politicians and thus had earned the respect of most cops. They were especially grateful for the substantial overtime and detail pay they got because of money she allocated for the department.

Judy did not cry. She didn't collapse onto Brady's chest. She never even glanced toward the kitchen where her son was dying on the family's floor. Instead she said simply, "My daughter shot my son."

It was the same message she had delivered during a 911 call at 2:22 p.m. "My son was shot," she had said. "I live at 46 Hollis Avenue." The call was so calm that for a minute the dispatcher thought it was a prank. Then she figured that the poor mother must be in shock.

Brady was stunned. He wondered where Amy was, why she wasn't on the porch with her mother, ready to explain away the accident. He didn't know yet that at that very moment, Officers Murphy and Solimini had tracked her to the Village News, where she would refuse to drop her loaded weapon, standing off against the cops with a shell in her pocket identical to the one that had dropped her younger brother.

"Why did Amy run out?" Brady asked. To himself he thought, *Why did she run out with her coat on? In the winter. That detail certainly made the shooting seem premeditated.* Judy paused to gather her thoughts before she answered the question.

"My daughter came into the kitchen carrying my husband's shotgun. I was at the kitchen sink and Seth was standing by the stove. She wanted to know how to unload the gun." She did not mention that Amy was wearing a blue winter coat.

"Amy said to me, 'I have a shell in the gun and I

don't know how to unload it.' I told her not to point it at anybody.

"Amy turned toward her brother and the gun fired, hitting him. Amy then ran out of the house with the shotgun."

Already the story had holes in it. Literally. For one thing there were two holes in the kitchen. One had hit the ceiling and blasted the plaster onto the floor. The other had ripped through Seth Bishop. Yet Judy Bishop only heard one shot, according to the police report. Upstairs in Amy's bedroom a vanity mirror had shattered. There were shotgun shells on her twin bed. The gun had clearly caused some damage not far from the kitchen. And Murphy knew enough about guns to be cognizant of the fact that a pump-action shotgun had to be re-racked with some power in order to fire twice. Maybe an accident could be argued with one shot. Murphy and others thought the story was completely implausible once there were two shots. And it was puzzling why Amy didn't drop the weapon. The recoil on a Mossberg 12-gauge shotgun would stagger a hulking man, never mind a petite woman.

Seth was loaded into the ambulance with Officer Rick Jordan riding alongside him in case he made any statements about the shooting, which was unlikely to say the least. He was unconscious and was sure to be pronounced DOA—Dead On Arrival—at Quincy City Hospital.

In the meantime, the crime scene unit detectives had arrived at the Bishop home. Quickly, they discovered something that the first responders had missed: the Mossberg 12-gauge shotgun had actually been fired *three* times. Detective Michael Carey had found that a blast had ripped through the wall in Amy's bedroom between her bed and a night table. The shot had broken a mirror and a lamp on the table. Amy Bishop had tried to hide the hole with a Band-Aid tin box and a book cover. A spent shell was recovered from the floor.

While Detective James Leahy took notes, Carey took a dozen pictures of the hole in the metallic wallpaper of Amy's bedroom and her attempt to hide the damage. He noted the broken mirror and lamp. He tossed the spent shell found on her bedroom floor into an evidence bag. He took another dozen photos in the kitchen where Seth was shot. A box of twenty-one shells was taken in as evidence from Judy and Sam Bishop's bedroom—where the gun was kept without a safe. Oddly, the cops vacated the crime scene and "left it in the care of a neighbor," according to the police report filed by Leahy. Not exactly police protocol to let a civilian neighbor hang out at a crime scene that had not been processed by the State Police CPAC unit, the squad that investigated homicides for the Norfolk County district attorney, Bill Delahunt. Then again, when it came to the police response to the incident, one could say that nothing made sense. Not the way the reports were written (every single one ruled the cause of death "accidental shooting" even before any investigation was launched), not the way the State Police said there wasn't any need for a trooper to respond, and certainly not the fact that Amy Bishop was allowed to go home that very night. All of those discrepancies were noted by Carey.

Leahy went back to file his report at the station and pulled out the Firearms Identifications, or FIDs, on file. In Massachusetts, the municipality where a resident lives determines who is issued a gun permit. In the liberal state, getting an FID card is no easy feat. So the Braintree Police were the ones who decided whether it was appropriate for the Bishop family to have weapons in their home. For most people who didn't, say, work in the diamond business or carry large sums of money, the answer was usually no. But the Bishops got their FID cards, which was perhaps no surprise given Judy Bishop's relationship with police officials. One card belonged to Seth M. Bishop, the other to Samuel S. Bishop. All of that was noted on the police report detectives filed that afternoon.

Sergeant Brady recalled being surprised that Judy did not create a commotion about getting into the ambulance with her son. He took her by the elbow and led her to an unmarked cruiser and they drove wordlessly to the hospital. Brady did not pepper her with questions. Sure, he wanted to know more, so he stuck by her side hoping something would come out of the seemingly impenetrable woman. He stood next to her in the emergency room. By then Sam Bishop had returned home from his Christmas shopping trip to the nearby South Shore Plaza shopping mall and found that his street had become a chaos of police sirens. He walked into his house and saw the blood-soaked kitchen floor.

"What the fuck happened in here? Is everyone all right?"

Leahy told him that his son had been hurt and ordered a uniform to drive him to the hospital. A nurse in the emergency room directed Sam Bishop to a room where his wife was waiting with Sergeant Brady and other cops. The couple did not embrace. Like his wife, Sam Bishop appeared to be in shock. Neither one had moist eyes. At 3:08 p.m. Dr. Thomas Divinagracia led the group into a private office and delivered the news. Seth Bishop had been pronounced dead. His initial cause of death was a ruptured aorta due to a gunshot wound.

At 7 p.m., an autopsy was conducted at Quincy City Hospital by Dr. William Ridder in the presence of a Braintree police detective. The autopsy concluded that

Seth Bishop was shot "from very close range" and that the blast ripped from the front to the back. The wound also contained birdshot pellets, the autopsy revealed. He lost too much blood to have possibly survived. The coroner made his ruling—"The cause of death was accidental pending police investigation"—concurring with the police reports, most of which were scribbled by hand seemingly in haste and dated December 6, 1986. Every one of the reports listed under the title *Incident:* "accidental shooting." The principal party named on the reports: "Bishop, Amy."

Three shots from a powerful shotgun were fired in a suburban Victorian home by a disturbed woman who then attempted to carjack several people. Three bullet holes—one hidden in her bedroom, one in the ceiling of the kitchen, and one buried in her younger brother's chest—and the incident was described as *accidental*. One cop remembers musing aloud, "Guess she accidentally pointed the thing at Solimini and Murphy too." At the time, many said the the handling of the case was preposterous. But it would take more than two decades for questions to be raised.

"My children got along well," Judy Bishop insisted to Brady. She said it repeatedly as they awaited word of Seth's condition. "I can't think of any reason why she would want to harm Seth."

Her husband Sam was silent. When he finally spoke he sucked in a deep breath and let it out. Then he uttered a single sentence. "Amy and I had a fight." To this day, Sam Bishop would not tell a soul what that fight was about. When pressed, he'd answer: "Just a fight."

The couple told police to bring their son's body to Mortimer N. Peck Funeral Home in Braintree. Judy looked at Sam.

"I'm going to the police station. They found Amy."

Her husband did not react to that information. Neither Sam or Judy went in to kiss their son's forehead to say good-bye. They did not collapse into each other's arms. "I lost one child," Judy said to no one in particular. "I'm not going to lose two."

It was a refrain she would repeat many times

Amy Bishop had been arrested at 2:45 p.m. Her brother would gasp his last breath twenty-three minutes later.

Sam stroked his beard and nodded. Sergeant Kenneth Brady offered Judy a ride to the police station. She accepted it.

By then Ronald Solimini—the arresting officer who had transported Amy Bishop to the Braintree Police Station, which was not far from the funeral home where her brother's body was about to be prepared for burial—had written out a police report in mix of cursive and block print, as if he was taking a pop quiz in the fourth grade. On it he simply wrote: "Sir, while transporting Miss Bishop back to the station after giving her Miranda rights Miss Bishop stated that she had an argument with her father earlier. Prior to the shooting, she stated! This statement was said in the presence of Officer Murphy and myself."

The report does not state what the fight was about. And apparently no one ever had a chance to ask Amy Bishop. Strangely, Solimini knew Judy Bishop already. She was one of the town politicians who had defended his father months earlier in a town issue over the retirement age. His father, Charles Solimini, had been fighting the town over the mandatory retirement age of sixty-five. He was fast approaching sixty-five, and felt strongly that he had another five years in him. Judy Bishop had testified that he should be allowed to stay on until he was seventy. "He's the youngest sixty-five-year-old I've seen in a while. He's not looking forward to retiring," Judy Bishop proclaimed. Ron Solimini remembered the exchange but had no idea that the nutty woman who had trained a shotgun on him was Judy's daughter.

Braintree Police Lieutenant James "Jay" Sullivan had Amy Bishop in the booking room.

"Amy, you understand you have the right to remain silent?" Sullivan asked her. She nodded to Sullivan and he continued to read her the Miranda rights he had memorized long before.

"You understand you don't have to talk to me?"

Amy nodded again.

"Want to tell me what happened?"

She took a breath and began. "I got into a spat with my father and I went to my room. I decided to load the shotgun because I was worried about robbers coming into the house. My father wasn't home."

Sullivan's eyebrows instinctively arched. He looked toward Ron Solimini. The cops exchanged glances at that one. Robbers in Braintree? Hollis Avenue, one of the nicest streets in the city, wasn't exactly a hotbed for home invaders, burglars, and other representatives of the criminal element. It was the type of suburbia so picturesque Norman Rockwell would have enjoyed painting it at Christmas.

"Did you know how to load the shotgun?"

"Seth showed me how to load it but not how to unload it," Amy answered. "I loaded it and it went off in my bedroom by accident."

"What happened then?" Sullivan asked.

"It hit a lamp and the wall. I tried to cover it up so my mother wouldn't see it."

"No one heard it? No one came upstairs?"

"Nope."

"Then what?"

Amy took her time to answer that question. "I went downstairs and asked my mother if she knew how to unload the shotgun. My mother told me not to point it at anybody. I turned and it just went off. It hit Seth."

Amy did not mention the second shot fired into the ceiling. Sullivan then asked her the question that had been weighing on every cop in the room.

"Did you shoot Seth on purpose?"

"No," Amy answered matter-of-factly. Not passionately. Not tearfully. As if Sullivan had just offered her a cup of tea.

Outside the booking room Sullivan heard a loud woman's voice. It was Judy Bishop. She had stormed inside the police station and yelled:

"I want to talk to John. Where is John? Where is JVP?"

Sergeant Ken Brady was stunned. He had never heard a single person refer to Chief John Polio by his first name. It was always Chief Polio. Maybe just Chief. Sometimes JVP—his initials. But never, ever did anyone refer to the boss as John. Not even his closest friends. If John Polio had any friends, which was unlikely. No one at the Braintree Police Department knew of anyone who would call John Polio a friend. Cops referred to him as a treacherous man. A man who many claimed would go out of his way to burn someone, especially an underling or someone who had slighted him—whether that slight was real or imagined. In fact, weeks earlier he had been called in to testify at a Town Selectman's meeting over a grievance that had been filed by his patrolmen. Some of those cops were in the room. According to these cops, when Polio was done testifying he turned around and wagged his finger at the officers. "I will get each and every one of you!" they said he barked. It was typical

Polio. If a cop, or a civilian for that matter, did not kow-tow to him, there was usually some payback. After that hearing, the patrolman claimed his "Polio files" on the union officials got fatter and the overtime and detail pay offered to those officers became nonexistent.

"Chief Polio is not here, Mrs. Bishop," Brady responded. He recognized her. He had seen her at town meetings. He later said he was afraid of what she was about to pull. "I'll take you down to Captain Buker's office."

Buker asked Bishop to wait outside his office and he dialed the chief's home phone number. He came outside, where Bishop was waiting with the sergeant.

"Can you give us a minute, Mrs. Bishop?" Buker asked. Then he nodded to Brady to step inside his office.

Judy Bishop did not wait a minute. Instead she stormed into the booking room where Jay Sullivan was interviewing her daughter—with Amy's consent. Brady followed her in.

According to Sullivan, Judy said, "Amy, shut up right now! Don't say another word. We are getting out of here. You are coming home with me. She's not answering any more questions. She is coming home with me. She is leaving here. Tonight."

This was unprecedented. Sullivan knew that Judy Bishop had some political pull in the town, but no one had ever stormed into a booking room in his police career and he was stunned. It took him a second to react.

"What is this?" Sullivan remembers asking. "You can't be in here." He looked at Brady. "What the hell are you doing in here with her?" He picked up the phone in the booking room and called Buker's office. Then, Sullivan remembered, he and his captain, D'Amico, went into Buker's office together. They did not want Judy Bishop privy to their conversation. Before the cops shut the door behind them, Judy Bishop looked at the officers and made another demand.

"Uncuff my daughter. Now."

Sullivan scowled at her. He would do no such thing. He left Amy Bishop handcuffed to the metal chair in the interview room. In the hallway Sullivan and D'Amico looked at one another. They were stunned. *Who does this bitch think she is? She has juice, but not that much juice. Who let her in the interview room in the first place? Why is Brady in there with her? There is a dead kid here.* In fact, Sullivan was convinced Amy Bishop had murdered her brother. He would be the only one to write the word "murder" on an official police document. It was on her booking sheet. That would later disappear.

"What the hell is going on?" Sullivan recalls demanding of Buker as he walked into his office.

According to Sullivan, Buker responded, "Calm down, Jay. This is coming from Polio. He wants her released."

"What? That's bullshit. This woman killed her brother and ran."

"I don't know what to tell you, Jay," Sullivan remembers Buker responding. "I just got off the phone with the Chief and he told me that Amy should be let go."

Polio later disputed any claims that he or his department had acted improperly. "The idea that it's clandestine . . . it's a cover-up is so outlandish it's ridiculous."

Buker, who would become a spokesman of sorts for the Bishop family in the days ahead, repeated the order that had been handed down to by Chief John Polio via telephone. The cops were flabbergasted. They had never seen anything like this.

"This woman is to be released into the custody of her mother," Buker said. "She's too upset to be interviewed." Then he directed every police officer involved in the case to write the incident up as an "accidental shooting." They did.

Sure, Braintree was not mired in violent crime in the late 1980s, so investigators did not spend a lot of time with "death invests"—the term for a potential homicide investigation until a medical examiner had ruled on a manner of death—but what Buker was claiming was a new one to them. *Too upset to be interviewed?* Since when did cops give a shit whether or not a potential perp was "too upset to be interviewed"?

As they wrote their reports, some of the officers shook with fury. Solimini mumbled under his breath. "This is bullshit. This is utter bullshit."

Sullivan was aghast. This woman had shot someone dead. This woman had tried to carjack a number of people. But most appalling, she had pointed a loaded shotgun at Braintree police officers. Their brothers. And she was going to walk out of the station without even having her mug shot taken. Without a booking sheet? Polio was crazy. This was absolutely, positively insane.

"What about Murphy and Solimini? She could have shot them! What about those people at the car dealership? The kids at the News?" Jay Sullivan peppered Buker with questions. He got no answers.

Sullivan had to resist the urge to shout. He was not going to let that crazy bitch Judy Bishop hear him. Clearly she had some influence with the Chief of Police in Braintree and even if he was dead against what was taking place that December night he could not afford to lose his job. He later recalled thinking that he would not put it past Chief John Polio to find a way to bounce him. Or, at the very least, make his life miserable.

Perhaps Buker felt the same way. He got to work seeing how the Braintree PD could make this case against

Amy Bishop go away. It would not be easy because the final determination on whether she would be charged did not rest solely with the cops who arrested her. The Norfolk County District Attorney, Bill Delahunt, would be the ultimate authority in the case. He had cracker-jack investigators from the Massachusetts State Police working for him in their investigations unit. One of those troopers was Detective Brian Howe. Howe was the trooper on call on that December night.

Howe would later say that Buker called him and said, "Brian. We have an eighteen-year-old dead here in Braintree. Looks like an accidental shooting. We can take care of the reports. I think we got this one."

That was another surprising move. The district attorney would make the final decision on whether or not a homicide had been committed in that bloody kitchen. Some Braintree cops felt Howe should have showed up regardless of what the small-town cops were telling him. But that's not how it works in a political place like Massachusetts. Howe was a foot soldier, not a decision maker. According to later testimony, phone calls were exchanged between Chief Polio and the top-dog prosecutors in Norfolk County, and Brian Howe was told there was no need to interrupt his Saturday. In light of the nature of the crime, *accidental*, Howe was told he would not be responding to the "secured" crime scene at 46 Hollis Avenue in Braintree. Secured by a civilian neighbor, that was. Trooper Howe had plenty to keep him busy so he didn't protest when his bosses told him he wasn't needed on this one. The cops didn't even process the crime scene before helpful neighbors came by and cleaned up the gory mess. One cop close to the family even stopped by to see if he could pick up any food to help with the mourning.

Even the press was kept off the story of a twenty-one-year-old shooting her eighteen-year-old brother on a wealthy street in a nice section of Braintree. The bigger papers, *The Boston Globe* and *The Boston Herald*, never reported the death at all. A short death notice, purchased by the funeral home and paid for by the Bishop family, ran in the *Patriot Ledger* on December 8, 1986. It was simple and certainly didn't hint at the kitchen bloodbath that had taken Seth Bishop's life. It read: *Bishop—of Braintree. [Died] unexpectedly. Seth Morrison. Beloved 18 year old son of Professor Samuel S. Bishop and Judith (Sandborn) Bishop. Beloved Brother of Amy Bishop . . .*

Unexpectedly? That's what Braintree police officer Paul Frazier thought when he read the local paper that morning. Frazier was home on administrative leave. He had been put on leave the day before, after his involvement four days earlier in a long police chase—always controversial in Massachusetts—involving a lowlife on the run from neighboring Holbrook. Frazier was on patrol with his partner, Tom Whitehouse, when the chase ended up in Braintree. Every cruiser jumped in. They chased the suspect roughly ten miles, all the way to Brockton. The suspect, James Threnholm, twenty-three, crashed into a house. Then he emerged from the car and pointed a rifle at Braintree cops. This was the first armed standoff of the week for the Braintree PD. The perpetrator fired a shot.

Frazier returned fire, shooting the suspect three times. The officers found a sawed-off shotgun and a knife in the dead suspect's jacket. Polio was pissed. A shot perp means a lot of paperwork, a lot of heat from outside agencies. He didn't need that. Besides, he never liked Frazier anyway. The two were often in a pissing contest. Frazier was a union rep, Polio a police chief. Frazier had defended his officers against the "angry prick," as some cops called Polio, many times. The day before the Bishop shooting, Polio told Frazier to stay home. He was put on administrative leave, which is standard after a police shooting, but Polio took a bit of extra glee in telling his rival to stay home. But Frazier's phone rang on Saturday night. One of the cops at the station was livid and wanted to report what was happening to the union official.

"This woman, she murdered her brother and Polio let her go," Frazier would later recall.

It was one thing to take care of a politician's parking ticket. It was another thing altogether to blow off an investigation into a dead teenager who had a promising future ahead of him before his chest was blown wide open by his very own sister. Frazier didn't buy the whole "accidental shooting" nonsense that Buker and Polio were pushing. No one fires a pump-action shotgun accidentally. Three times.

The first news story of Seth Bishop's "accidental shooting" did not appear until Monday, two full days after he had been pronounced dead. It was a front-page story in the *Patriot Ledger* on December 8, 1986:

Sister kills teenager in shotgun accident at home
BRAINTREE—An 18-year-old who won prizes in science and music was killed when his sister accidentally fired a shotgun she was trying to unload in the kitchen of their Braintree home Saturday afternoon.

Seth M. Bishop, a freshman at Northeastern University in Boston, was shot in his home at 46 Hollis Ave., at about 2:20 p.m. Saturday, police said.

Police said his sister, Amy Bishop, was trying to unload the pump-action, 12-gauge shotgun when it discharged.

The fatal shooting was witnessed by Bishop's mother, Judith, according to authorities.

The shotgun was registered to Bishop's father, Samuel S. Bishop, a professor at Northeastern University.

According to investigators, Amy Bishop had been taught how to use the shotgun by her father. On the day of the accident, she was handling the loaded weapon in the home, although investigators said it was not clear why.

She pumped a round from the magazine into the firing chamber of the shotgun, then went into the kitchen and asked her brother and mother for help when she couldn't eject the shell from the chamber, investigators said.

Her mother instructed Amy Bishop to pump the shotgun again, which ejected the first shell, according to an investigator. However, she apparently pumped the weapon again and unknowingly advanced a second shell from the magazine to the chamber.

Thinking the weapon was empty, she pulled the trigger, the investigator said. The blast struck her brother, who was standing three to four feet in front of her, authorities said.

Dr. William P. Ridder, an associate Norfolk County medical examiner, said Bishop was shot once in the lower right chest with bird-shot. . . . Dewey said Amy Bishop, who graduated from the high school two years ago, was also a talented violin [sic] who had gone on to study at Northeastern.

"They were very much alike, shy and pretty much out of the mainstream."

And the story would stay that way. Out of the mainstream. Amy Bishop went home. The Bishop family began to plan Seth's funeral. The cops wouldn't even come back to 46 Hollis Avenue—or talk to any member of the Bishop family—for eleven full days.

On December 12, 1986, the *Patriot Ledger* ran another story on the shooting. Captain Theodore Buker, the man who had ordered Amy Bishop released, offered the same information. The whole sordid mess was merely an unfortunate accident. In fact, he backed up the family's tale of a burglary at the home a year earlier. But no police report was ever dug up on that event.

Gun fired moments before teen's death

BRAINTREE—The shotgun that accidentally killed an 18-year-old college student in the kitchen of his Braintree home Saturday had gone off moments before in an upstairs bedroom.

After she accidentally discharged the gun into her bedroom wall, the victim's sister, Amy, carried the weapon downstairs and asked for help unloading it. It was then that the shotgun discharged a second time, fatally wounding Seth M. Bishop, police said.

"It all happened in a split-second in front of me," Judith Bishop, their mother, said this morning. "I keep seeing it over and over in my mind."

Mrs. Bishop said Amy was trying to teach herself how to use the 12-gauge shotgun in case burglars broke into the house. The family purchased the gun after their Hollis Avenue home was burglarized a year ago, Mrs. Bishop said.

When the shotgun went off in her bedroom, Amy Bishop, 20, [sic] became frightened and "highly emotional" and went downstairs to her mother and brother to find out how to unload it, Braintree Police Capt. Theodore Buker said.

"She came downstairs to the kitchen seeking help

on how to unload it," Buker said. "Her mother said something like, 'Be careful where you point that' and as she turned around (toward her brother) the gun discharged."

Seth Bishop, a 1986 Braintree High School graduate and an award-winning violinist, was struck in the lower chest by the shotgun blast.

His funeral was today at All Souls Church in Braintree and he was to be buried later today in Exeter, N.H. He was a student of electrical engineering at Northeastern University in Boston.

Mrs. Bishop said last year's burglary was followed by an attempted housebreak[ing] just before Thanksgiving. Buker confirmed those incidents.

"I think she (Amy) thought she should know how to use it in case she was home alone," Mrs. Bishop said. "She didn't know anything about it."

Buker said after the gun went off in her bedroom, Amy Bishop apparently pumped a second shell into the firing chamber, then went downstairs seeking help. He said she probably did not know she had advanced a second shell into the chamber.

"It is not an automatic weapon, so in order for the shell to be advanced, it would have to be pumped," Buker said. "It isn't particularly hard to do."

Buker's comments clarified a report in yesterday's *Patriot Ledger* which said Amy Bishop tried to unload the shotgun by pumping it and had ejected a shell, but inadvertently loaded a second shell into the firing chamber and pulled the trigger.

Both Buker and Mrs. Bishop said Amy Bishop did not try to unload the weapon because she did not understand how it worked.

After the incident, Amy Bishop ran from the house with the weapon. Police officers found her a short time later near Braintree Square in a "highly emotional state."

Samuel S. Bishop, the father of Amy and Seth, was not at home at the time of the accident, Buker said.

Again not so much as a word about the standoff Amy Bishop engaged in with the police.

No mention of her attack on two men at the old Dinger Ford car dealership. No mention of the neighbor who had been menaced by Amy as she fled out of her house. Even more curious, no one thought to mention the *National Enquirer* article that described the 1986 murder of the parents of Patrick Duffy, who starred in the TV series *Dallas*, that lay spread out on the floor of Amy's bedroom. The couple had been shot dead at the bar they owned in Montana by two teen thugs.

The story, titled "*Enquirer* World Exclusive—Chilling Details of the Night Patrick Duffy's Folks Died," lay on the floor, not far from the spent shotgun shell, beneath the hole she blasted through her bedroom wall, a shot that her mother would steadfastly deny hearing in the family's old home.

No one thought much of the *Enquirer* piece after Seth Bishop was shot dead. The story would become part of a much larger look into what happened on December 6, 1986, more than two decades later.

4

"I never saw a young man with such a strong sense of family," Debbie Kosarik would tell a young reporter for a free weekly newspaper published in Braintree in December of 1986. "He cared about each one so much."

She was speaking of Seth Bishop, the young man who had died "unexpectedly"—according to death notices the family paid for in local newspapers—on December 6, 1986. One neighbor after another began to share stories about Seth Bishop, about the manner in which he cared not only for his parents and older sister but about his neighborhood as a whole. There was the time neighbors spotted him under his father's car securing a loose muffler with old twine. There was the inevitable scrape of his shovel against the driveways of the elderly after a snowstorm. There were the classmates who he tutored in math, for free, to help them pass. There were the trips to the supermarket he made for a woman on Hollis Avenue who was too old to drive. Teachers at the Colbert and Hollis elementary and junior high schools remembered his kind spirit and extraordinary math and music skills.

Even his sister weighed in on the story that ran on December 18 in the *Braintree Forum & Observer*. The family had not spoken to investigators yet, but they did speak to a reporter. In fact, Judy Bishop even gushed, "You cannot believe how kind the Braintree police were to us." The newspaper neglected to mention that Amy was the one who caused Seth's death. The story did not contain so much as a sentence on how Amy Bishop, now grief-stricken sister, had in fact been placed under arrest, albeit briefly, for the "unexpected" loss of the eighteen-year-old virtuoso violinist.

"He knew physics even when he was seven years old," Amy Bishop told the reporter. "He would go to the town hall and get a map, first in Braintree, then when he was older, in Holbrook and Braintree. He would map out a route and follow it on his bike. The point was to cover as many streets as possible," she recalled. "One day when he was about seven and I was with him, I fell down a small cliff and couldn't get up. He knew even then that if he spread his body in a certain way that he could add strength and pull me up.

"He saved my life that day."

Days after the shooting she would describe her brother as a "calm, giving, funny brother who was always there for me."

Amy Bishop did more talking to a small-town newspaper reporter than she would do with police. In fact, Braintree Police Detective Michael Carey, his boss Captain Theodore Buker, and State Trooper Brian Howe, who did not respond to the scene of the crime but was responsible for the official report on the case, did not visit the Bishop home until December 17, eleven days after the killing. By that time the case had been assigned a number, 864718, and the incident was being described as "Shooting at 46 Hollis Avenue."

Cops believed those eleven days gave the Bishop clan ample time to get their story straight, so that the time line matched. They contended, for instance, that their house was "very soundproof," which explained why the first shotgun blast fired by Amy Bishop went unnoticed by her mother, Judy, who was home at the time. The word "accident" was repeated over and over again. Police reports suggest that investigators seemed to help the Bishops along with their version of events. There were no probing questions about why Amy fled from the home with her coat on. No one was grilled about the "family spat" that had been mentioned on the afternoon of the shooting. It seemed that crime scene investigators did not even bother to mention the trajectory of the shots to see if Amy's version matched the forensic evidence. The bullet hole in the ceiling of the kitchen—separate from the one that hit Seth—was never mentioned in the report at all. Evidence was not collected. Fingerprints were not taken. Even the shotgun was returned to the family when Amy was released. It remained unclear whether the shot into the ceiling was fired before or after Amy fled the house.

The reports typed up by Detective Michael Carey were very carefully worded. No one at that time expected that the case would ever make it to a grand jury, never mind be scrutinized decades later. Carey started the questioning that day with Judy Bishop. She described a normal morning.

"I went to the stables at 7 a.m. Everyone was home. I came back and asked if there was anything for lunch. Seth was home and went to the store because there was not anything for lunch. He brought groceries back into the kitchen.

"When he was unloading the groceries, that's when Amy came down the family's winding wooden staircase and around the corner into the kitchen with her father's shotgun. It was not aimed at the floor, either.

"She asked me if I could help her unload the gun. I

told her not to point it at anyone. Amy turned and the gun went off and hit Seth."

Judy screamed and Amy ran out of the house. Judy admitted that she did not comfort her dying son but instead called 911 and went out on the front porch to wait for police.

"I knew he could not live," she said, as if that could explain how she could leave her beloved son to die alone. Even when police arrived and tried desperately to save Seth's life, cops would later remember Judy remained on the porch with that eerie, calm stare.

Carey asked her about the first shot fired from the powerful Mossberg pump-action shotgun. "I didn't hear it," she said. "The house is very soundproof." Again, no question about the hole in the ceiling in the kitchen from the second shot. Or third shot. It would be impossible to determine which shot was fired when because the crime scene was not professionally processed.

Carey had questions of his own and made hand-scrawled notes to himself. "Upstairs bedroom found one spent shell on the floor between bed and the wall by the nightstand . . . Reason to keep shotgun in home?" He also wrote: "Did anyone hear the shotgun blast in bedroom before the girl came downstairs?" Most notably, Carey was befuddled as to why "girl had her jacket on?" He wrote, "Unusual to walk around with jacket on."

The interview then turned to Samuel Bishop.

"I wasn't at the house," he said. "I left at 11 a.m. to go shopping at the South Shore Plaza."

When Sam left, he waved to Seth, who was washing his Camaro. Amy was in the house and Judy would be home any minute.

"I had a disagreement with Amy about a comment she made," he said. "She went to her room."

Again, the investigators did not ask Sam what the

argument was about. Or whether the tiff was over a comment she made about Seth. Or whether she stormed to her room in a rage, angry enough to grab his shotgun and blow holes through her bedroom wall, into the ceiling of the kitchen, and into her brother's chest. At least the answers to those questions never became part of the official police record into the shooting at 46 Hollis Avenue. Instead, the questions were steered toward the gun. Where did it come from? How was it stored? Where did they fire it? Did Amy have any prior experience with it?

Sam Bishop told investigators he bought the gun at the Coleman's in nearby Canton, Mass., a year earlier. He said he would take Seth to the Braintree Rifle Club so they could bond as men. He said the gun was stored, unloaded, on top of a trunk in a rifle case in his upstairs bedroom. The bullets were on the bureau in the bedroom.

"Amy didn't know how to use it," he said. Then he stood up, looked around the room, and walked out. He was a college professor teaching students at an expensive private college. He was an artist, a respected filmmaker. Cops felt he had airs on that day, like a man who didn't wish to be interrogated by blue-collar civil servants. He apparently did not appreciate people prying into his family's personal business. Before he shut the door, leaving his wife and daughter with the investigators he uttered a final sentence. "I don't have anything else to add. I have said everything that there is to say about this."

The final interview took place with Amy herself. The major players were there: Detective Howe from the State Police, Captain Buker, and Detective Carey, who would write the report.

Amy stated that on the morning of the shooting her

mother had gone to the stables and her father went shopping. She added that she did not know where her brother Seth was, Carey wrote in his report.

Amy told investigators she was in her room when the thought suddenly occurred to her that she would go into her parents' bedroom and learn how to load her father's shotgun. No one asked her why she didn't wait for her dad to get home from the mall or why she didn't call for Seth, who did in fact know how to use the weapon.

"The gun was on the chest," she said. "The bullets were on the bureau. I put the shells in the gun. I couldn't get them out. I tried unscrewing the bottom. The gun was on the bed and it just went off," Amy Bishop told investigators.

They asked if her door was open or closed—as if that could explain why her mother didn't hear the powerful report of a shotgun pull in Amy's bedroom. "I think it was open," she said. "I was beside my bed near the door when the gun went off."

Any law enforcement officer with even the most basic knowledge of weaponry should have immediately raised an eyebrow at the idea that a shotgun lying on a bed could go off on its own. A Mossberg 12-gauge shotgun is a powerful weapon; firearms experts say it takes significant pressure on the trigger—anywhere from five to five-½ pounds—to release a round. The mere loading of the gun makes a racket that her mother should have heard it from the kitchen. The barrel was 18-½ inches long, and when Braintree cops grabbed Amy there were two 12-gauge Remington Field #4 rounds in the magazine holder. Moreover, the gun is used by police departments and the military, so the cops would have likely fired one at some time during their training to get on the force. Even if they hadn't, the officers could have asked someone and learned that it takes a distinct action to grasp the forearm, or the slide, of a pump-action shotgun and rack it back to eject a round—like the one Amy Bishop claimed spontaneously fired from her bed. For a second round to be ready, there is a second forceful motion to rack and load another shell. Loading the gun is not only a laborious project, it's a loud one. Hard to believe no one in the house heard the *Whack! Whack!* of the gun being readied.

As if that weren't enough, Amy told the cops she didn't "recall" whether she put another bullet in the gun after it went off. It was obscene that cops would believe that nonsense. Amy had to physically rack another round into the gun and pull the slide back with some force for it to be ready to be fired again. It is hardly a weapon with a hair trigger. It takes five pounds of pressure to unleash the gun's fury. Not something that happens haphazardly.

"I think my mirror got broken and there was a hole in the bedroom wall," she said. "I heard Seth come in and I went downstairs to ask him for help. I was carrying the gun pointed down beside my leg. Seth told me to point it up. Seth started walking across the kitchen between me and my mom. I had the gun in one hand and started to raise the gun. Someone said something and I turned and the gun went off.

"Seth said, 'Oh God.' And my mother began to scream. I thought I ruined the kitchen so I ran out the back door. I thought I had dropped the gun when I ran."

What about the neighbor who said Amy had pointed the shotgun at her? What about the men at Dinger Ford? What about the tense gunpoint encounter with Braintree cops and the teenagers working at the Village News?

None of it was mentioned in the police reports written up by Carey. Those criminal acts weren't even mentioned in the interviews with Amy.

"I don't remember anything until my mother came to the police station."

The cops did not ask her a single question about her statement, as implausible as it was. For one thing, there is no possible way that a woman, or most men, could hold that weapon with one hand and run out the door with it after it was fired, as Amy Bishop claimed. There is a such a forceful recoil, a violent kick, that if she really had been holding it with one hand it would have flown out of her grasp and could even have broken her wrist.

Her version of events, which included repeated claims that she was worried about "robbers" and that she had heard stories of "what happens to people" during home invasions, was taken at face value. Though the investigators knew firsthand that it was patently false, Amy "also stated that she did not cover up the hole in the wall of her bedroom," Carey wrote. No one pressed her on it.

Now the case was in the hands of Trooper Brian Howe and the Norfolk County District Attorney's Office, which was run by a politician named William Delahunt. Delahunt, a longtime friend of the Kennedy dynasty in Massachusetts, also had connections to John Polio, the Braintree Police Chief who considered Judy Bishop a friend. Whether or not Amy Bishop would be charged with a crime for any of the offenses she committed that winter afternoon, and whether a competent police investigation could come up with a plethora of felony assault and menacing criminal charges, would lie solely in the hands of Delahunt. He was the man who would have to convene a grand jury, present evidence, and lock up the woman who very clearly had killed her brother. Then, at trial, a jury or a judge could determine whether or not she was guilty. Under Delahunt, the case would never get that far.

Howe took his time writing up his case report. He dated it March 30, 1987—nearly four months after Seth Bishop bled out on his family's kitchen floor. The report was addressed to first assistant District Attorney John Kivlan, one of Delahunt's top dogs as far as prosecutors went. The subject was Accidental shooting of Seth Bishop, white male, D.O.B. 4/9/68 at 46 Hollis Avenue, Braintree, Massachusetts on December 6, 1986." The report would come to cement what many in the Braintree Police had already come to accept: The department was going to "deep-six" the case, cop parlance for burying a criminal investigation. Buker would be the cover-up guy and Howe was going to have to tidy it up with a report on the case even though he had never even visited the crime scene.

> . . . the preliminary investigation conducted . . . indicated that the victim had been shot by his sister Amy Bishop, and that the apparent cause of gunshot discharge into the victim had been accidental in nature. Captain Buker further stated that indications were that Amy Bishop had been attempting to manipulate the shotgun and had subsequently brought the gun downstairs in an attempt to gain assistance from her mother in disarming the weapon.
>
> During her attempt to disarm the weapon in the kitchen of her residence, the weapon had apparently accidentally discharged, resulting in the fatal wound inflicted upon her brother.
>
> Captain Buker further stated that at the time the discharge occurred, Judy Bishop, the mother of both the victim and Amy, had been in the kitchen and had

witnessed the entire incident. Judy Bishop had indicated to the responding officers that the discharge had been accidental in nature and that the discharge had occurred while Amy was attempting to unload the weapon.

Captain Buker also stated that Amy Bishop had fled the residence immediately upon discharging the weapon and had subsequently been located by Braintree officers and brought [to] the Braintree Police Department for questioning.

Captain Buker stated that due to the highly emotional state of Amy Bishop, it had generally been impossible to question her while she was at the Braintree Police Department relative to the circumstances of the firearm discharge, and that as a result of these facts, she was thereupon released to the custody of her parents with further investigation to follow at a future time.

This officer therefore determined that due to the inability to question the witnesses at that time as a result of their highly emotional state and their inability to recall specifically the facts relating to this occurrence, as well as the fact that Judy Bishop stated that she had witnessed the entire affair and the discharge had been accidental in nature, it was determined that additional interviews would be conducted at a later time, allowing witnesses to stabilize their emotions. . . .

Arrangements were subsequently made to conduct interviews of all of the members of the Bishop family . . .

Amy stated that she was not aware of any additional facts which could assist these officers in their investigation into the death of her brother and she reiterated adamantly the discharge had been accidental and that she was still having a very difficult time dealing with what had occurred and was currently under medication with a doctor's care.

As a result of these ongoing facts, a meeting was conducted between this officer, Captain Buker, and Detective Carey. It was determined that due to the testimony of the members of the Bishop family and, in particular, the testimony of Judy Bishop relevant to the facts concerning the death of Seth Bishop, that no further investigation into the death of Seth Bishop was warranted.

It was therefore determined that the cause of death of Seth Bishop would be listed as the accidental discharge of a firearm in the possession of his sister, Amy Bishop, and that the investigation would be concluded."

In hindsight, an average man off the street wholly unfamiliar with the ins and outs of law enforcement could have given that report an even cursory read and suspected that a cover-up had taken place. The police work was astoundingly shoddy from the start. The crime scene was not secured. Evidence was not processed. Police reports were titled "Accidental shooting" that very evening. Amy was released without even going through the booking process. Investigators did not interview a single person in the Bishop family until eleven days after the killing. Cops never again interviewed the men at Dinger Ford who were threatened by the frenzied woman with the shotgun and did not bother to list those at Village News who witnessed the standoff with Amy Bishop and police. It was highly unusual that witnesses would not be interviewed because they were "emotional." It was ridiculous to believe that "inability to recall specifically the facts" about the shooting would be a valid excuse when there was a dead teen with a promising future in question. It was unconscionable to suggest that witnesses to that killing would be allowed "sufficient time to stabilize their emotions."

But the larger question was this: why would so many men of power—police officials, prosecutors, state troopers—take such an extraordinary risk for a disturbed twenty-one-year-old woman whose mother was part of a system that had minimal control over the purse strings of a small police department on the South Shore of Massachusetts? That answer would be clear to anyone familiar with what is often referred to as the "hackarama" in Massachusetts. Politics in the Commonwealth operated like an organized crime family in some ways. Politicians took care of the people who held fundraisers, who swayed votes, by securing jobs on the state payroll that came with a guaranteed sweet pension at the taxpayers' expense, or by getting someone "out of a jackpot"—which referred to police trouble.

Back then and in the two decades that followed, it would seem inconceivable that it would ever come back to bite them.

5

"All politics is local," the late respected Massachusetts Congressman Thomas "Tip" O'Neill once declared, and William Delahunt was the type of man who took that sentiment to heart.

He grew up in blue-collar Quincy, Massachusetts, listening to stories from his grandfather Thomas, a Boston police officer, about how important organized labor unions were going to become in the United States. His own father, Bill Delahunt Sr., was a hardworking sales manager, and his mother, Ruth, was a homemaker. Before he could even ride a bike, young Bill Delahunt knew that any politician worth his or her salt would unfailingly support the men on the front lines. Delahunt's grandfather had experience in such matters. Bitter experience, in fact. In 1919, the Boston Police Department—the nation's first—also became the first group of public safety officials to strike because of the deplorable working conditions the officers experienced daily. Police stations were vermin-infested hellholes. Officers were forced to work shifts so long and grueling that it wasn't uncommon for some to collapse from exhaustion. There was an influenza epidemic raging in the city, and police were sent into the homes of the sick without any protection against the illness. Veteran cops decided that they needed representation.

When the time came, most of the force voted to join the American Federation of Labor, seeking higher wages and better working conditions. The police commissioner, who reported to Republican Governor Calvin Coolidge, refused to allow his rank and file to unionize. Republicans ran Massachusetts in those days. On September 9, 1919, most of the force—1,115 officers, including Bill Delahunt's grandfather, Thomas, one of the organizers of the strike—refused to show up for work. The entire force deserted its post. Chaos ensued. Looters wreaked havoc. Over the next several days, nine people would die in riots, with no cops to respond to the mayhem. The National Guard was called in to quell the violence. In the end, the strike accomplished nothing for the cops. Officers who had served the city for decades were served with pink slips from the then-governor, who went on to become the 29th vice president, and then the 30th president of the United States. Thomas Delahunt, father of six, found himself out of a job after twenty years in blue. Coolidge would be far from the Bay State's last Republican governor of Massachusetts, but after the Boston Police strike, the GOP would never again control the House of Representatives or the State Senate.

It was into this world that Bill Delahunt was born, on July 18, 1941. All of that anti-Republican sentiment was drilled into young Bill's head early on. "That's why I became a Democrat," Delahunt frequently remarked. "It was the Republicans who fired my grandfather."

In the Delahunt household in Quincy, the mere mention of Republican politicians was enough to send the elder Bill Delahunt into a rage. It was understandable.

Delahunt's father had grown up watching his dad become despondent at the loss of a job he had held for twenty years. The family struggled financially. The tough old cop's ego took a beating. And the union-busting Republicans were to blame. Back then, the Republican Party was viewed as anti-ethnic with a special grudge against Roman Catholic newcomers from Europe, including the Irish, who made up the majority of the Boston Police force. In the eyes of the Boston Irish, Republicans were out for themselves. They were a party comprised of rich WASPs, the type who hung signs in business windows that read IRISH NEED NOT APPLY. It was very rare for Catholics to support Republicans. They'd be as likely to vote for the Queen of England. Some parents would have stamped a *D* for Democrat on their kids' birth certificates, if they could have.

Delahunt would spend his life making sure no one would have control over him the way politicians had held sway over his grandfather. His parents managed to muster up the money to send him to the exclusive Braintree private school, Thayer Academy. For his mother, going to an elite private school was a good start to getting into an Ivy League school. She envisioned her strong son Billy working as a doctor or a dentist. Private school would begin the path. Or so she thought. Delahunt never excelled as a student. Before long it was clear that there would not be a Delahunt strolling the leafy campus at Yale or through Harvard Yard. Bill Delahunt instead went on to earn a bachelor's degree from Vermont's Middlebury College in 1963. It was there that he became involved in the Democratic Party, as the Co-Chair of the Students for John F. Kennedy organization. It was a savvy move to get involved in politics around the time of the Kennedy dynasty, especially for an

Irishman who hailed from the South Shore of Boston, a stronghold for the Kennedy clan, which had set up a compound on the shores of Cape Cod in Hyannis.

It was also at Middlebury that he met his stunning wife Katharina Elfriede Hermani, a first-generation German woman whose parents immigrated to the United States from Hamm. The handsome couple got married in 1966. Katharina was pregnant with their daughter, Kristin, while Delahunt was a law school student at Boston College, an institution run by the Jesuits, and an incubator for Irish-Catholic power in Boston and beyond. In the early 1970s, Kristin would get a little sister. This was during the Vietnam War, and the Delahunts were by then deeply immersed in politics. In 1975, during the controversial Operation Babylift, they went so far as to adopt a daughter who had been orphaned in Vietnam. The couple was anxious to welcome their new daughter when there was news that a U.S. Air Force C-5A Galaxy transport plane overcrowded with Vietnamese orphans had gone down shortly after leaving Tan Son Nhut airfield, near Saigon. Many of the 243 children aboard the aircraft perished in the crash. The couple panicked. For hours they sat by a radio and waited by the phone for news from Vietnam. Then the call came that the daughter they had never seen, but whom they had already fallen in love with, was on the next carrier out of the war-ravaged country and would be arriving in Boston in a matter of days. In a move that the couple had frequently described as the grace of God, Kara Mai had been moved onto a plane set to take off right after the one that went down. Pronounced a miracle baby by her new parents, she was four months old when she became a Delahunt. Kara would provide the inspiration for her father's future legislation on international adoption issues.

By the time Delahunt got out of BC Law, he was wired politically. He had a very powerful friend: John F. Kennedy. Delahunt had gone from supporting the future President's campaign to befriending JFK's brothers Robert and Edward "Teddy" Kennedy. "It was a very exciting time," he told a reporter. "In the 1960s there was the civil rights movement, the Vietnam war, the era of Jack Kennedy, Martin Luther King. I was swept up in the sentiments of those times. That government could do good, could change things."

The Kennedys would also help Delahunt realize there were few jobs in Massachusetts more secure than that of a Democratic politician. His decades on the public payroll began in 1972 when he was elected to the Quincy City Council. He loved that the City Council chambers were directly across the street from the Church of Presidents, where John and John Quincy Adams are both buried. Soon, however, the politics of a small municipality like Quincy proved boring. In 1973, Delahunt was elected to the state legislature. His ambition was growing. Before Delahunt had a chance to author any legislation as a state lawmaker, he had already launched a campaign to run for Norfolk County District Attorney. It is very difficult to knock out an incumbent district attorney, and Delahunt knew it. It was also a job that paid fairly well, carried a better public profile than his current job, and didn't require a lot of heavy lifting. The key was to hire decent prosecutors who put away enough bad guys to garner helpful headlines portraying the DA as a crime fighter. Those headlines were money in the bank for district attorneys with greater political aspirations. And every DA in Massachusetts had greater political aspirations.

In 1975, with a valuable assist from the Kennedy clan, Bill Delahunt became the District Attorney of

Norfolk County, making him the top lawman on the South Shore of the Boston metropolitan area. It didn't take long for him to embroil himself in controversy. When he did, it came as little surprise to the prosecutors working under him. They often lamented the fact that the boss would clearly rather play golf or take power lunches with campaign donors than get into the messy daily work of putting away bad guys.

One such bad guy was Myles J. Connor Jr. who would become linked to the powerful district attorney in ways that would follow Delahunt for decades.

Connor was a one-man crime wave, a notorious art thief who has long been suspected of involvement in the infamous heist at the Isabella Stewart Gardner Museum in March of 1980. In that case, two men posed as Boston police officers and talked their way into the museum by telling guards they had received an alarm call. Once in, they handcuffed the two on-duty security guards and went to work. By early morning the thieves had stolen 13 works of art valued at over $500 million, including *The Concert,* one of Johannes Vermeer's thirty-five known paintings, and three works by Rembrandt van Rijn, including his only seascape, *The Storm on the Sea of Galilee*, and a small self-portrait print. They got works by Degas, Manet, and Govaert Flinck, as well as two objects: a Chinese Ku, or beaker, and a finial from a Napoleonic flag. Even today it is considered the biggest art theft—and property theft—in history; the crime remains unsolved. The museum still displays the paintings' empty frames in their original locations, in accordance with the strict provisions of Gardner's will, which required that the collection be maintained without a single change.

Connor's career as an art thief began in 1966, when he was twenty years old, with a robbery at the Forbes

House Museum in Milton. During a pursuit, he shot and wounded state police corporal John J. O'Donovan. Shooting a state trooper is a crime that ordinarily would elicit a long jail sentence, but somehow Connor managed to get a sympathetic parole board to let him out of prison in 1972. His freedom would be short-lived. He was rearrested in 1974 for stealing several artworks by Andrew Wyeth from the Woolworth estate in Monmouth, Maine. He pleaded guilty but avoided jail by working as a confidential informant for investigators looking to orchestrate the return of a $1 million Rembrandt, a painting that had been stolen from Boston's Museum of Fine Arts in broad daylight. No one ever went to jail for the theft and it never became clear if Connor himself had a piece of the action.

Connor's name surfaced again in connection with the murder of Boston Police Officer Donald Brown, who was shot dead while escorting a supermarket manager to make a deposit. Three men pulled up and ordered the manager to hand over the day's take from the store. Brown, who was working a paid detail, reached for his service weapon and was shot dead. The sixty-one-year-old Boston police veteran was murdered on the job just six months before he planned to retire to Florida with his wife. Once again, Connor managed to stay out of prison, even though he had been fingered as an accomplice in that case. He was never charged.

In 1981, a jailed hit man, Thomas Sperrazza, turned state's evidence and accused Connor of orchestrating the 1975 screwdriver killings of two eighteen-year-olds, Susan Webster and Karen Spinney—both witnesses to a murder in Roslindale linked to a Connor associate. It was a horrifying case. The girls had been on a date with Thomas Sperrazza and his pal John Stokes. The guys had picked the girls up at Webster's house, and after a few stops out on the town they ended up at a Roslindale bar. Inside, an argument broke out between the two mob associates and a random patron. It started with exchanged insults, escalated to punches, and spilled outside. Standing on the sidewalk, Sperrazza pulled out a gun and shot the patron dead. Stokes came outside and emptied the clip of his own gun into the victim just in case. Susan Webster stood outside screaming. She refused to get back into the car with the men she had just witnessed murdering a stranger. So they pulled her in and the car screamed away from the scene. Karen Spinney was so shocked she got in the car wordlessly. The girls were seen later that night being pulled into a basement apartment in Quincy that was rented by friends of Sperrazza.

"Get outta here for a while," Sperrazza told them, according to court documents. When the couple returned, their apartment was splattered with blood, and a sleeping bag and a knife were missing. The teenage girls were never seen again. Their bodies would not be found for nearly three years, not until Myles Connor led investigators working for District Attorney Delahunt to a wooded area in Northampton, Massachusetts, where the teens' skeletal remains were found along with a sleeping bag and knife exactly like the items reported missing in Quincy. No one seemed to ask Connor how he knew where the bodies would be located. Connor would later come up with a tale of how he convinced Sperrazza during a jailhouse visit to draw up a map—an unlikely story.

Sperrazza turned state's evidence after he was charged with those murders (among four he was convicted of) and fingered Connor as the man who came to Quincy and ordered the teens killed. He told investigators that he had handcuffed Susan Webster in the bedroom and Karen Spinney in the bathroom. Then he called Connor.

Connor told him to shove a screwdriver into the girls' temples and twist—which Sperrazza said he did. Then Connor helped him and Stokes dispose of the bodies in western Massachusetts. Connor's name along with his mother's Milton address were discovered scrawled in the register book at a hotel near where the bodies were found. The entry was dated the night after the Rosindale shooting. And a jury bought Connor's story. The prosecutor who tried Connor was right: "Who's the schemer here?" Paul Buckley said dramatically, pointing at Connor. "Who's the one putting this all together? That man right there. The leader of the band."

On March 20, 1981 Connor was convicted of ordering and directing the murders. It was a relief to every cop and prosecutor in the courtroom—some even stifled smug smiles—when Connor was handcuffed and taken to MCI-Walpole state prison. Oddly, his verdict was overturned on a technicality in 1984 by the Supreme Judicial Court. The SJC—the state's highest court—is made up of judges who are appointed to the bench by politicians. Their ruling was a strange one. A juror had been dismissed from the jury, which the SJC said prejudiced the case. The judges did not explain how the dismissal would have provoked a guilty conviction, but nonetheless Connor was a free man. Again. It wouldn't be the first time the SJC sprang a maggot in a politically charged case. And it wouldn't be the last. A search of campaign donations made by members of the judiciary almost always turns up large checks written to the coffers of politicians with the most power.

Connor was retried for the teenagers' murders in 1985, but jumped bail hours before being found innocent by a twelve-person jury. He was quickly apprehended and given a year in prison on the bail-jumping charge. It was the maximum time allowable.

Connor, who is still considered one of the most prolific art thieves in the world, grew up in Milton, not far from Delahunt. More importantly, though, he was the son of a Milton cop—a cop who had worked very hard on cases for Delahunt's office. Throughout Connor's bloody run, there were accusations of cover-ups. How else could one guy have gotten away with so much mayhem? Every time he was connected to a jackpot— even the shooting of a state trooper or the murder of a Boston police officer—he got off or was given a light sentence. It left a lot of cops baffled, even the ones who respected Connor's father, the decorated Milton police officer. People wondered whether Connor had a friend in law enforcement. It took the Sperrazza case to identify that friend as none other than Bill Delahunt.

It was Delahunt's office that was charged with investigating the murders of the teenage girls, because the homicide had taken place in Quincy, part of Norfolk County. By then, Connor was a confidential informant playing a cat-and-mouse game with the feds trying to negotiate the return of stolen art. Some believe Delahunt liked taking credit for helping big shots on the board of the Museum of Fine Arts, and he liked dealing with the rock star art thief who had played with the hot group Sha Na Na. Connor was, by all accounts, a valuable informant, and valuable informants help district attorneys make big. He was also garrulous and funny and brilliant, a descendant of the Mayflower who was a Mensa member, so as far as informants go it was much easier to hang out with a guy from the neighborhood who cracked jokes and hung with rock stars than the scumbag druggies and gangbangers who usually played the rat game in the state prosecutors' offices. Connor's band, Myles Connor and the Wild Ones, had played with the Beach Boys and Ray Orbison. For an accused cop killer, Connor maintained an eclectic assortment of friends on both sides of the law. And many saw Delahunt as one of the art thief's protectors, including some in the Attorney General's office and the U.S. Attorney's office.

With Sperrazza in the witness protection program protected by the feds and crowing about Connor, Delahunt at one point during one of the bank robber's many retrials was called to the stand by his informant's defense attorneys. The district attorney testified that Sperrazza had no credibility and was "perhaps the most vicious killer in the history of Massachusetts criminal justice." True. But Connor was no better, just better protected, many cops believed. And Delahunt had already infuriated law enforcement figures by making a call to Karen Spinney's mother, saying, "There's going to be a search for your daughter's body in Northampton. Don't tell the Boston cops." Delahunt actually conducted that search with Connor on September 14, 1977, according to Myles J. Connor's own autobiography, *The Art of the Heist*. Yes, not only did the guy get off a number of times for serious crimes, he got a book and movie deal. In the book, Connor insists he knew nothing about the murders.

When Spinney's mother talked in court about the call she received from the district attorney, it brought the tensions simmering between Delahunt and the Boston police—who had connected the Roslindale bar shooting to the teens' disappearance—to a boil. During one of the Connor trials, some cops told reporters that Delahunt had gone so far as to threaten to arrest them if they went after his prized informant for the double homicide. Assistant U.S. Attorney Edward F. Harrington was livid. He went to the press to castigate District Attorney Delahunt for abusing his power. This was an extraordinary thing—ordinarily those sorts of interagency law enforcement beefs were kept behind closed doors—but Delahunt wasn't worried. Harrington was a fed, an outsider. This was Boston. Delahunt, on the other hand, was an insider. He had political muscle and state house juice—primarily from his lifelong friend William "Billy" Bulger, a rising star in the Massachusetts House of Representatives who had the distinction of also being brother to James "Whitey" Bulger, the sociopathic kingpin of the Boston mob. There is no evidence that Delahunt was concerned by the fact that Connor was sometimes known to associate with the criminal-minded Bulger brother.

Apparently Delahunt didn't give a rat's rear end about the feds. He would be just fine, he told friends. And he was right. When Connor was finally brought to trial in 1981 by a special prosecutor appointed by then-Massachusetts Attorney General Francis X. Bellotti, Delahunt was accused of harassing four Boston cops and two state parole officers who had worked on gathering information to help convict Connor. Then-Boston Police Commissioner Joseph Jordan took a public swipe at the Norfolk County District Attorney during a press conference, and told reporters at the *Boston Globe* and the *Boston Herald* that Delahunt's motives to protect Connor "were unclear." But accountability has never managed to take hold in Massachusetts politics. Even the Ethics Commission, a twenty-person panel that costs state taxpayers millions every year to maintain, rarely admonishes any elected officials for ethics violations. Delahunt often ran unopposed, so the voters were not demanding answers. He knew the bad headlines would eventually be forgotten. And, once again, he was right.

It was during that trial that the fractured relationship between Delahunt and other law enforcement agencies became glaringly apparent. At the trial, Connor's attorney even called Delahunt to the stand to testify to Connor's sterling record as an informant, which he did. During his testimony, Delahunt admitted to cutting deals with Connor that granted him early release from prison. It didn't help. Connor was convicted in 1981. By then, Assistant United States Attorney Edward Harrington was so angry at Delahunt that he wrote to Attorney General Bellotti to demand an investigation into the relationship between the Norfolk County District Attorney and the career con art thief. Cops were livid that even after Connor was convicted of murdering the girls in 1981 Delahunt continued to insist that he was innocent, and would get his way four years later when Connor's guilty verdict was overturned.

That wasn't the end of Myles Connor's career in crime, however. His name kept turning up, even if a charge never stuck. It came up in connection with the 1984 theft of the Massachusetts Bay Colony Charter and its beeswax seal from the basement of the state house. Cops later found the charter page (along with $200,000 worth of Oriental rugs) during a raid at the apartment of a Dorchester woman who had been known to be romantically involved with Connor.

All of it made Delahunt the scourge of some Boston police. A lot of detectives and staties hated Delahunt. But he didn't care. He was one of the beautiful people in Massachusetts politics. He had frequent invites to the Kennedy compound. The maître d's at the city's priciest restaurants recognized him upon entry and reserved power tables for his lunches and dinners. He was such a ladies' man that his wife divorced him in 1986, sick of the stories of her husband's dalliances outside their marriage. None of the rumors or the scowls thrown Delahunt's way bothered him. He didn't need people to like him. Power was much more important than popularity. And Delahunt had it.

Once again, Delahunt escaped any real consequences. He was like the Teflon politician. None of the criticism leveled against him—even befriending a murderous man who was believed to be a cop killer and who was convicted of shooting a state trooper—ever affected him at the polls.

So when a *Patriot Ledger* reporter whom Delahunt was "close to" was found dead in her apartment after a blaze, there were no political ramifications. He was questioned about his relationship with the woman in 1981 but he was never cited for any wrongdoing. The investigation into the reporter's strange death was closed with no charges filed. Three years later the *Boston Herald* would report that Delahunt had asked investigators to keep his testimony in that investigation secret.

There were further questions raised about the way Delahunt handled the 1989 murder of Susan Simoni, a mother of three whose family owned a flourishing florist shop on the South Shore. Simoni was thirty-seven years old when she was shot twice in the face in her Jeep. Her husband, Brian—wealthy and politically connected—was considered the prime suspect. He had a gun, and when cops asked him for it, they found that two bullets—the same type used in the murder—were missing. His wife belonged to one of the wealthiest families in Norwood. There had been some marital discord reported. But no charges have ever been brought and the case went cold. Some cops believed that Delahunt had only been protecting himself. He had been seen dining with Susan Simoni and he did not want that sort of dalliance with a married woman to be revealed. It wouldn't look good, especially for a divorced guy looking to run for higher office. It would take years for the District Attorney's Office to present a case. No suspects. No leads. No one was ever pursued. By then, Delahunt was on his way out of the Norfolk County prosecutor's game. He was eyeing Capitol Hill as a member of the United States Congress and would soon mount his first run.

So while the complaints against Bill Delahunt mounted over the years, none of it mattered. He was untouchable. For twenty-two years he ran the DA's office, accountable to absolutely no one. No one even bothered to run against him, so his campaign war chest did not have to be spent battling an opponent. He spent it on lavish meals and trips. When reporters clamored for his tax returns throughout his twenty-year career as the district attorney in Norfolk County—a standard public record that most politicians released without any fanfare—Delahunt steadfastly refused. According to the *Boston Herald*, campaign finance records showed that he had spent more than $10,000 on meals at expensive restaurants and even vacationed at Hedonism in Jamaica, an adults-only retreat popular with swingers and fetishists, using cash from his campaign war chest. His wife had never accompanied him on those trips to Jamaica.

When there was a problem, it was easy to blame John P. Kivlan, the hardscrabble prosecutor he put in charge of the big cases, while he sat back and plotted his next political move. Kivlan had an impeccable reputation and took on each case—especially the homicides—personally. He knew his squad spoke for the dead. Delahunt was lucky to have him. It was easy to hide when there was a good prosecutor in charge.

After all, Delahunt had always been more of a politician than a prosecutor. That much would become abundantly clear years later, in the Amy Bishop case.

6

One afternoon in the winter of 1987, Jimmy Anderson Jr. opened the front door to his parents' Foxboro home and stepped inside. His mother, Sandy, was cooking dinner in the kitchen when she heard the door open. Her husband, Jimmy Sr., was at work at Honeywell, and not due home for a while, and Jimmy Jr. was supposed to be off at Northeastern, where he was a student. She was surprised to see him.

It wasn't like Jimmy to be spontaneous, but something took hold of him that winter day in 1987 and he jumped on a train from Boston to Mansfield, and then took a bus to his childhood home in Foxboro, his girlfriend in tow.

His parents had heard about the girlfriend, but they hadn't met her, didn't know anything about her family. Jimmy had been dating her for a year, but had never invited his parents to Boston to meet her, never brought her by for holidays or anything like that. She was a biology student, like Jimmy. And smart like Jimmy, only a little strange. She was big into that Dungeons & Dragons nonsense. Just like their boy.

Sandy Anderson looked up to see a pretty, stout woman with flowing black hair and piercing eyes. She didn't say a word, the girlfriend. She just evaluated

Sandy with a strange stare. She seemed very tightly wound. The girl made Sandy nervous.

"Mom," Jimmy said, "this is Amy."

Amy looked up and nodded. "Nice to meet you."

Jimmy went upstairs to grab something, leaving the pair in the kitchen. There was an awkward silence between the two women. Sandy Anderson was southern, naturally garrulous and affectionate, and she instinctively moved to embrace her son's girlfriend. When she did, she felt Amy stiffen. The young woman wasn't used to hugs, and certainly was not accustomed to having a stranger's arms wrapped around her. After the brief embrace Amy looked at her boyfriend's mother.

"Let me go find James," she said. And when she did, they left. It took more than an hour to get to the Andersons' on the South Shore of Massachusetts, and Jimmy and Amy spent less than a half hour there before heading back into the city. Sandy was so struck by the odd encounter that she called her husband at work to describe it.

"Jim needed something in his room," she recalled. "She stood there and looked at me." Sandy sounded indignant. The girl wasn't just shy; she was abrupt and unfriendly. Sandy had a generous spirit and was willing to give Amy the benefit of the doubt, but this was too much. "Honestly, she was rude," Sandy told her husband. "There is something not right about that girl."

Sandy had no idea how right she was. It had only been a few weeks since Amy had killed her brother. Jimmy never mentioned a word of it. There had been a family funeral at All Souls Church Unitarian Universalist Church in Braintree, and Jimmy was there. The line of mourners on that cold day so close to Christmas stretched into the street. Many wept openly. A eulogy was delivered by the Reverend Otis Oakman, while Jimmy and

Amy sat next to her parents in the front pew of the church. Amy was a mess. At one point she had to be held up by her parents. She was hysterical. Jimmy was standing next to her when she bid good-bye to Seth at a cemetery in Exeter, New Hampshire.

Yet Jimmy Anderson didn't breathe a word of any of this to his parents. Perhaps because he didn't know exactly what had happened himself, except that there "had been an accident." He didn't press Amy for details; she never offered any. Her parents had never been warm or welcoming. He guessed that whatever happened in the Bishop household, it was none of his business. He had met Seth a few times, liked the kid. Knew he was popular on campus at Northeastern. But they had not become buddies or anything like that. As for his parents, he had essentially cut them off. Sure, he'd call once in a while to say hi. But that was it. His life was about Amy now.

Before Amy and Jimmy Anderson left Foxboro that strange winter evening, there was one thing that his mother took note of. No one had ever called her son James. It wasn't his name. When he was born on March 9, 1964, the name on his birth certificate was Jimmy Anderson—Jimmy being an Anglicized version of Demetri. Like his father, the younger Jimmy was named for a man named Demetri, a Greek ship captain who had grown up alongside the elder Anderson's own father in their native Greece. The two were cousins but were more like brothers. Demetri was a family name and Jimmy Anderson Sr. was going to honor his Greek heritage even if his parents had brought their children up as Americans—red-blooded, patriotic Americans no less. Still, Demetri had been like a brother to the elder Anderson and when Sandy got pregnant for the first time he knew he would name his son Jimmy. Just as his father had named him Jimmy.

But Amy had repeatedly called him James. "Let me find James," Amy had remarked to Sandy. "James, are we ready to go?" "James, did you get your bag?"

Even the way Amy said it, a little snootily, gave Sandy pause. The Andersons had never been an uptight family. Her husband was a beloved Boy Scout leader with Troop 32 in Foxboro. Sandy was a den mother in Cub Scouts. The Andersons were given to hosting backyard barbecues with their neighbors and would not have been comfortable at cocktail parties with bookish academics like the ones Amy had grown up with, thrown by her arts professor father. The Andersons liked to read books, sometimes trashy ones, and watch comedy sitcoms on TV, while Sam and Judy Bishop raised their children with no television sitcoms, only art house films, and nothing but science books. Sandy did not have a problem with the idea that Amy Bishop came from a classy, educated family. But Sandy would never forget that stiff hug she exchanged with her future daughter-in-law that day. It would be the last time there would ever be any physical contact between the two women. Every time there was even the threat of affection, Amy would pull back, turn her cheek. She didn't even like to shake hands. Jimmy Jr. would explain that Amy was "germaphobic."

"She's a scientist. She knows what's out there," he would quip.

To hear Amy refer to her son as "James" seemed ominous to Sandy Anderson. It was as if the name change was an indication that the Andersons had lost their son. She felt like Amy had taken her son away. In a way she was right. Before long, Jimmy—James—would give up his postgraduate studies and move into a Harvard University dorm with Amy Bishop. He gave up his name. He gave up his studies. He gave up frequent contact with his family. The relationship would do much more than dampen the younger Anderson's identity. It would nearly land him behind bars.

7

James Anderson married Amy Bishop on August 20, 1989 at the very same church where her brother's funeral mass was held just three years earlier: All Saints Universalist Unitarian in Braintree. Both had graduated from Northeastern University a year earlier. Even after Seth's death, Amy did not interrupt her studies. She had always been industrious and driven. What held her back was a complete lack of social skills. Fellow Northeastern University students remembered Amy as standoffish, a loner. "She didn't know how to make small talk. She was utterly and completely invisiblo," a classmate, Isabel Gomes McCann, would tell a *Boston Globe* reporter. At the same time, Amy craved fame and attention. She didn't reach out to classmates, but she wanted to be noticed nonetheless. "She didn't like being invisible. It made her angry," McCann said. "But in the scientific realm she was noticed. People listened to her."

She had graduated cum laude and had completed an honors thesis titled: "The effect of temperature on the recovery of sea lamprey from full spinal cord transsection" that caught the attention of recruiters at Harvard University.

The couple had initially moved into a dorm room at Harvard University so Amy could pursue a Ph.D. in genetics while Anderson worked on projects of his own. It was unclear who proposed first. James Anderson would later tell his parents that one day he was living with his girlfriend, then next thing he knew he was being dragged to the altar.

Amy told James that he could act as the househusband and take care of their eventual children while engaging in his own independent research. She also told him that he had to always use the name James Anderson. At the same time, she refused to take his last name, looking forward to the day that she would be referred to as Dr. Amy Bishop. It would make her parents proud, and there was no way she was going to be a scientist with a nondescript name.

It was an odd wedding, Jimmy Anderson Sr. would later remember. First of all, just as his wife had been startled to hear Amy call their son James rather than his birth name, Jimmy, it was jarring to "hear the preacher call my boy James. That was not his name."

After watching his son kiss his bride, Anderson shook his hand and asked him, "Son, what's with James? Your name is Jimmy."

"Amy thinks it's more acceptable. She doesn't want people to think I am a southern redneck. James just sounds better. She's in Harvard, Dad."

And from that day forward, Jimmy Anderson Jr. insisted that everyone in his life call him James. He would use it in banking. He would use it for business. He would identify himself in every area of his life as James Anderson. He did it for Amy.

His father was not happy about it. Not at all. In fact, he was not thrilled about the wedding. He immediately disliked Sam and Judy Bishop. He thought they were stranger than their daughter. He had never seen such a cold clan in his entire life. He thought that Amy was trying to build his son into someone he was not to fit into her fantasy life as a scientist.

"It was like she was trying to build a robot," the elder Anderson would say. "I was not happy about that wedding at all. She had no past. We didn't know anything about her. We didn't know what their future was going to be. They were living in a dorm room. We barely had any contact with my son. It was like she was keeping him away from all of us."

But the worst part about the wedding was the way that the Bishop family ignored the Andersons—even during the reception. Not a single person approached their table during dinner. There had been a very swift introduction before the nuptials were exchanged. After that nothing. Not a word. An uncle came over and shook hands with Jimmy Anderson Sr., but it was such a curt hello that to this day he can't remember the relative's name. If it bothered Sam and Judy Bishop to be in the same church where just three years earlier they had said good-bye to their dead son Seth, neither of them showed it. Just as they had been the night he died, the couple was stoic. There were no exchanged glances of pride when Amy slipped her husband's ring on his finger and said "I do." There were no tears when their daughter was pronounced married. Just terse smiles. The Andersons thought they seemed above all emotion. They did not engage in the same sentiment as normal families. It was almost as if they felt superior to everyone around them.

"There were big alarm bells going off in my head. The whole thing seemed like a staged event, like the 'making of Amy Bishop.' I didn't like it one bit. I didn't like the way my wife and I were ignored. I didn't like the way that everyone was calling my boy James. I didn't like how snobby the people in the Bishop family were,"

Anderson would later recall. "It was impossible to get to know that family. Sam. Judy. Amy. The whole lot of them were weird as hell. They were hiding something, but we had no idea what it was."

The fading relationship the Andersons shared with their son before the marriage only got worse, even after Amy and "James" had their first child, Lily. Sure, they got the phone call announcing her arrival and were mailed pictures, but James Anderson and Amy Bishop did not travel south to show the Andersons their grandchild. It was the same story when their other two daughters, Thea and Phaedra, were born. It was not until 1993, when Amy Bishop had garnered some fame at Harvard University for some of her research, that Jim Anderson Sr. heard from his son.

James and Amy Bishop were in trouble, big trouble. The Bureau of Alcohol, Tobacco, and Firearms was asking all kinds of questions about a letter bomb that was left on the doorstep of one of Amy Bishop's bosses, a doctor and researcher who taught at Harvard University. The Feds told James Anderson that they had a witness who had heard him say that he wanted to kill his wife's boss at the neurobiology lab at Children's Hospital.

"Dad, I think this is bad," Anderson remembers his son saying.

The former Jimmy Anderson Jr. was right. It was bad.

8

It was six days before Christmas in 1993 and Paul Rosenberg and his wife had just gotten back from a vacation in the Caribbean. They always tried to travel in December. They lived near a shopping center in Newton Highlands Village in Newton Highlands, Massachusetts, and the neighborhood was a perpetual traffic jam around Christmas. Holiday parties made it hard to get a table at any of the nearby restaurants. Plus, they were both exhausted by the end of the year. Rosenberg was a neurologist at Children's Hospital, where he had worked since 1979; a senior associate in the Neurology Department at Children's Hospital Boston; a staff physician in the Department of Neurology at the Beth Israel Deaconess Medical Center; and an associate professor teaching neurology at Harvard Medical School. He specialized in sleeping disorders in children and cerebral palsy. His schedule was intense and stressful. His wife, Harriet Moss, was no layabout either. She worked as an attorney at the Executive Office of Communities and Development. It was a state job that came with good benefits and a pension. She had long been involved in Democratic politics and had donated to politicians in the party. Moss didn't make a boatload of money, but she was giving back to under-privileged neighborhoods and cities across the common-wealth.

The couple had no children at home but did have a number of cats. Before they left on vacation, they called a pet service in Belmont, an upscale neighborhood where even feline sitters are subjected to rigorous back-ground checks. Every day for a week, a woman from the service named Brooke Cutler would arrive at the Rosenberg home on Standish Street to feed the cats and collect the mail. On December 19, she found a simple white cardboard box behind the storm door, addressed to Mr. Paul Rosenberg, MD. The return address read: "Union of American Hebrew Congregations. 1330 Brook-line St., Brookline, MA 02146." The cat sitter took it inside and left it on the kitchen table.

Standish Street in Newton Highlands is a posh ad-dress, and the cops who responded to the 911 call about a mail bomb on December 19 knew it well. There was massive response. There were troopers from the Mas-sachusetts State Police Bomb Squad; special agents from the FBI and the ATF showed up, along with U.S. Postal Police. It was a rare thing to see a Dutch Colo-nial in Newton Highlands crawling with cops and agents, but there was a very good reason for it.

At that time the FBI was immersed in what would remain to this day one of the lengthiest—and most expensive—investigations in that agency's history. They were hunting a man who had come to be known as the Unabomber. This man got his name from the FBI task force—UNABOMB—that was charged with investi-gating a string of explosives that had been sent to uni-versities and airlines. By the time of the Rosenberg 911 call, the Unabomber had mailed 14 bombs. Many people had been hurt, and one had died as a result of the bombs.

One bomb forced an emergency landing of a Boeing 727 en route to Washington, D.C. when it began smoking in the cargo hold (the bomb didn't go off).

Each bomb the Unabomber sent was more sophisticated than the one before. It started in 1978 with a bomb sent to Northwestern University. No one was injured. Another was mailed a year later to the University of Illinois at Chicago; it injured a campus cop. That same year, the Unabomber tried to take down the American Airlines flight. In 1980, Percy Wood, the President of United Airlines, seriously burned and cut his hands opening a package sent to his home. Two years later, in 1982, a bomb was defused at the University of Utah in Salt Lake City. No one was hurt. But a secretary at the Vanderbilt University in Nashville, Tennessee, would not be so lucky. Janet Smith's arms were blown to bits. She would undergo years of therapy. So would a professor at University of California at Berkeley. Diogenes Angelakos would suffer wounds to his face and hands after a letter bomb blew up in his office. A year, later a graduate student at Berkeley named John Hauser would lose four fingers and the sight in his left eye. In fact, the Unabomber would send five bombs in 1985 after Hauser was critically wounded. On December 11, 1985, there was an explosion at a Sacramento, California, computer rental store that killed its owner. It was unclear why that victim, Hugh Scrutton, was targeted. In 1987, the owner of a Salt Lake City computer store, Gary Wright, would nearly lose his arm. In 1989, a geneticist named Charles Epstein at the University of California, San Francisco, blew out both eardrums and mangled three fingers opening a Unabomber package. Two days later, David Gelernter, a Yale University computer science professor, suffered injuries to his right hand and right eye.

Thus far, the UNABOMB Task Force hadn't been able to find the perpetrator. Not with 150 agents. Not with all the resources made available by the newly elected President Bill Clinton. Not with all the shrinks and investigators and bomb techs they had working the case. The guy was a genius. He never left so much as a fingerprint. He was a ghost.

The return label on the package on the Rosenbergs' coffee table read, "Union of America Hebrew Congregation. 1330 Brookline St., Brookline, MA 02146." It looked like the label had been made on a standard laser printer. The congregation was a real one, in the words of the organization, dedicated to "providing means for the relief of Jews from political oppression and unjust discrimination and for rendering them aid for their intellectual elevation." The address was also real. It was an office building near the bustling Coolidge Corner neighborhood of Brookline.

Rosenberg was not expecting any mail from the group, however. He wasn't all that religious. He was, however, careful. This Unabomber business was scaring the hell out of academics across the country, and he was no exception. Universities had been warning professors what to do in the event that a suspicious package materialized at their homes or offices. Rosenberg grabbed a butter knife and carefully opened the package in the middle, not at the seams. Cutting the seams would detonate the bomb. Bomb techs called these devices "victim activated," because ordinarily the way they were opened triggered the explosion. Rosenberg cut into the box and held it at arm's length. He spotted wires and a metal pipe and yelled to Harriet.

Rosenberg called 911 from his house phone and then went to get Harriet who was upstairs on the opposite side of their six-room home.

"I think I just got a bomb in the mail," he told the operator. "It is a suspicious package and there appears to be some sort of device inside."

It took less than a minute for the first officers to arrive. The street was closed off. Rosenberg and his immediate neighbors were evacuated. Residents who lived a little further away were told to stay inside and keep away from the windows. The Feds came not long after, including members of the UNABOMB task force. Bomb squad techs assigned to the Office of the State Fire Marshal pulled on their bomb suits. One tech examined the package. Inside were two pipe bombs about six inches long attached to two nine-volt batteries. The tech noticed a pressure-activated switch. If Dr. Rosenberg had opened the box at the flaps, it would have exploded in his hands. It was powerful enough to kill him and probably would have injured his wife.

One of the pipe bombs was brought outside onto the front lawn of the Rosenberg estate. Bomb techs, still wearing their protective suits, conducted a controlled detonation of the first bomb with what they called "a disruptor"—a machine known as a detonating cannon. Paul Rosenberg and Harriet Moss were kept behind a protective police line. Instinctively their hands clapped the sides of their ears at the *boom* that sounded when the explosive was rendered safe by the bomb squad. The second bomb was left intact and transported back to the Office of the State Fire Marshal. From there it would be sent to a lab run by the postal inspectors in Washington, D.C. The two pipe bombs were almost identical in size and strength. Both were four and a half inches long and one inch wide, wired with micro-switches and powered by four nine-volt Sears-brand batteries. They were stuffed with black powder and finished off with four snap connections that activated two switches. The makings of the bomb were common enough. It was the knowledge of how to put it together that would lead investigators to their suspect. It took someone with some engineering expertise to design such a device.

Dr. Paul Rosenberg was a lucky man. But there still remained the disturbing question of who wanted him dead. So the investigation began. Trooper Howard K. Eaton was assigned to the case, along with Postal Inspector W. C. Mastrangelo of the Boston office. Both men were explosives experts. Bureau of Alcohol, Tobacco, and Firearms special agent Bill Murphy would soon join them.

What about patients? Any strange patients?" Eaton asked.

"I work mainly with children. I can't think of anyone associated with my work at Children's who was angry with me for anything. Not enough to want to kill me."

There was a flyer, Rosenberg remembered, a piece of literature from a kook and perennial presidential candidate named Lyndon LaRouche. LaRouche—a self-described fascist who believed that Jews, gays, and the British are the catalysts for all the problems in the world—sent flyers to the largely Jewish Newton residents that claimed the Anti-Defamation League was a front for a drug cartel. The couple looked at it, laughed, and stuffed it in the trash.

Rosenberg also told investigators that he shared his name with another doctor who worked in women's medicine. That doctor had met a woman on vacation and she had tried to track him down by calling every Dr. Rosenberg in the book. Sometimes a lunatic would mail him a ranting missive at the hospital. But there were never any direct threats.

But then, there was something else, Rosenberg said.

"A friend of mine lives down the street. He told me that he saw a small red car, maybe a Honda, with a guy handing out the anti-Jewish Defense League stuff," Rosenberg said.

Harriet Moss held her husband's hand. It was nerve-racking to think how close they had been to death. Certainly everyone in academia had been nervous about the victims of the Unabomber. She was shaking, but remained composed. It was unlikely that she was the target, she knew, but she was still racking her brain to think of any strange encounters she might have had in recent months.

"What about you, Ms. Moss?" Eaton asked. "Everything okay in your workplace? Anyone threaten you?"

"I'm just a lawyer. I have been there since 1987. I haven't been involved in any controversial cases," Moss answered. "I'm a housing advocate. The people I deal with are elderly people, minorities, who are looking for low income homes. It's not a position where I am making people unhappy."

The investigators were fairly certain it was not a Unabomb and let the couple know that night. Still, it was sent to the lab. In the lab in D.C., investigators had determined that the remaining pipe bomb was made differently than those recovered at the scenes of the Unabomber attacks. It didn't take them long. The Unabomber case was the top priority for the Clinton Administration's Department of Justice. The bomb was processed by the end of the week. Judging from the components used, the report noted, "FBI has ruled out UNABOMB involvement." Rosenberg was not a target of the domestic terrorist they had been hunting since 1978. By the time the FBI reached this conclusion, two more bombs had been mailed. Both were fatal. (When the Unabomber was finally captured at a remote cabin in Montana in 1996, Ted Kaczynski had killed three people and wounded another twenty-two.)

Instead, investigators had narrowed their focus to one of Dr. Rosenberg's students and her husband. That came after Rosenberg called Trooper Eaton that week and told him that weeks earlier he had terminated a young woman who had worked in his neurobiology lab at Harvard Medical School. The woman had been working as a postgraduate research fellow, and Rosenberg had "played a role in her resignation," he gently told police. He said he thought the woman "could not meet the standards required for work" in his demanding lab. Worse, she was on "the verge of a nervous breakdown," after learning that her postdoctoral work would not receive a glowing review by Dr. Rosenberg, her boss. "Her husband can't hold down a job," Rosenberg told investigators. "She has shown violent, unstable behavior."

Her name was Dr. Amy Bishop, he said. Her husband was James Anderson.

"I had to give her a negative evaluation," he told the cops. The woman's reaction to the evaluation had nagged at him. It was immature, sure, for a grown woman to become so angry at a review. But there was more than that. She seethed. It had made him nervous. She had actually intimidated him a bit.

"She didn't like that."

Dr. Amy Bishop didn't like that one bit.

9

Dr. Paul Rosenberg sat at his kitchen table with the two lead investigators charged with finding whoever had tried to kill him. Bill Murphy was a veteran agent of the Bureau of Alcohol, Tobacco, and Firearms. His counterpart in the postal inspector's office was Bill Mastrangelo. The men had worked together before. As a matter of fact, their fathers had worked together in the post office. The state police had turned the case over to the Feds.

Murphy and Mastrangelo were compiling a list of people who had a grudge against the Harvard professor, or maybe even his wife. Rosenberg had had more time to think about who might want him dead. There was a child he was treating whose mother did not want to pay a bill. There was that abortion doctor he was sometimes mistaken for because they had the same name. But Rosenberg was nagged by the suspicion that the one person who both had the wherewithal to pull something like that off, and was unstable enough to try, was Amy Bishop, the strange woman who had worked in his lab. Rosenberg was supposed to advise her on her thesis and his input would be a big part of her overall evaluation. Therein lay the problem. Bishop was a perfectionist. Her professor was about to tell people at Harvard that she was not perfect.

"Amy quit on November 30, 1993," Rosenberg told the agents. "I had been instrumental in her leaving because I felt she could not meet the standards required for the work."

Rosenberg was not the only one worried that Amy Bishop was unstable. "I felt like she had problems with depression. So did a lot of other people. She was not a stable person. She is married to a man who had trouble holding a job and who was working in a field where he tinkered with machines. . . ." Or built pipe bombs, was the insinuation.

"Over the years there was a growing concern over the behavior of Dr. Bishop. She has exhibited violent behavior," Rosenberg said.

After news broke about the bombing attempt, one of Rosenberg's colleagues had approached him and said that she was afraid Bishop might have been the one who tried to hurt him. That woman, Sylvia Fluckiger, had worked with Amy Bishop. She did not find it a pleasant experience.

"We knew she had a beef with Paul Rosenberg," she told investigators. "No one thought it was a coincidence that he would get those bombs after she left."

Apparently, Bishop believed that Rosenberg was going to take credit for some of the research she had conducted in his lab. She had complained, loudly and crazily, some believed, that Rosenberg "wanted to jump on the train and take over the engine." There had even been a confrontation with Amy Bishop over other students usurping her space. She was arguing with other lab assistants, saying that they were trying to take credit for her work. Rosenberg urged Amy Bishop to move on, saying that he was running out of grant money to soften the blow. Something had told him he did not want a confrontation with her. He went as far as to urge Bishop to attend a meeting that he had set up for after he returned from his Caribbean vacation. They could discuss her future. Rosenberg was even willing to write her a letter of recommendation.

Murphy and the postal inspector began to dig into Bishop and Anderson. They clandestinely followed them and began to interview people close to them. One of those people was Donald Proulx, who had grown up in Foxborough with Anderson. The two had remained friends. When Anderson was having problems with a neighbor, he asked Proulx to circumvent the strict Massachusetts gun laws and buy him a gun. Proulx told the Feds he had helped out his friend by picking up a handgun at a store in Troy, New Hampshire, just months before. It was a 9-millimeter P85 semiautomatic Ruger. Proulx volunteered that information to the federal agents. But there was something else. It related directly to Paul Rosenberg and the letter bomb.

"James Anderson told me he wanted to get back at the guy," Proulx told the agents, according to ATF records. "He said he wanted to shoot him, bomb him, stab him, or strangle him."

With that, the case of the letter bomb, now called investigation 63213-94-0024 D, had officially named James Anderson and Amy Bishop "principals" or lead suspects, in the case.

Bill Murphy was a dogged investigator. He had been with the agency since 1976 and was an influential player already in the Joint Terrorism Task Force. His appointment came long before the nightmare of September 11. He had been investigating gunrunning by terrorist organizations for decades by then. The IRA had been prevalent in Massachusetts. In fact, Boston Irish raised more money for "The Cause" than the Irish in Belfast. Guns were Murphy's specialty. He was the master at tracing guns that had their serial numbers scratched off, supposedly making them untraceable. He also knew a thing or two about bombs, and after looking into Anderson's background, he concluded that this guy was certainly capable of fashioning a letter bomb. Anderson had a background in chemistry and engineering. He was a "tinkerer," as he liked to tell friends.

Murphy started his background checks in Foxboro, Massachusetts, the town where Anderson and Proulx grew up. The Andersons had had problems with the neighbors that lived alongside them on Alden Street, where they had lived since 1975. They relocated from Alabama to Foxboro after Jim Anderson Sr. landed a job at Honeywell, a tech firm located in the nearby town of Acton. The Andersons were beset with prejudice. "Our home was egged often," the elder Anderson would remember. "Our mailbox was set on fire. They didn't like people from the south." There was an altercation that got ugly after Anderson told a group of kids who he claimed were harassing his children, "if you don't cut the crap, I will beat you so bad your own mothers won't recognize you." The police were called. Reports were written.

Murphy and Mastrangelo thought it might be a good idea to start their shoe-leather investigation on Alden Street. That's where they heard about Troop 32 of the Boy Scouts. The boys in it could earn a merit badge for handling antique firearms, which used black powder exactly like that found in a pipe bomb. Troop 32 was run by Jimmy E. Anderson Sr., the suspect's father, and another man named Arthur Butler. James Anderson and his buddy Don Proulx were both Eagle Scouts and had earned the merit badge for handling antique weapons. There were purchases of black explosive powder that were traced back to the troop. Boy Scout Leader Arthur Butler never forgot the day he was questioned by ATF special agent Bill Murphy. He was called to the Foxborough police station to answer questions about the purchase of the black powder.

The Rosenberg case had been all over the news, so Butler was aware of it. He just never thought he would wind up a part of it. "They tried to make it sound like the troop was being turned into, I don't know, some kind of radical organization to make bombs," Butler recalled to a local paper, the *Sun Chronicle*. "At this point I had to laugh. They had a strong suspicion it came from someone associated with the troop."

Murphy asked him repeatedly about the Andersons. What were they like? Did they have any enemies? Butler was getting angry. "He kept questioning me in the same vein. I was getting fed up. He was like a dog with a bone in his teeth. He wouldn't take no for an answer. I said as far as I know, there's no black powder at all anywhere."

Then they moved on to Jim Anderson Sr. The elder Anderson told investigators he was teaching some new skills to his Boy Scout troop. He would joke about it to anyone who would listen: "Can you believe they thought *I* was the Unabomber? Goddamn it. Me? Old Man Anderson?"

"They got this wild suspicion that I was the Unabomber. They put two and two together and came up with six. Then they thought my Jimmy tried to kill that professor. They got it in their twisted mind. The Unabomber used black powder. There was black powder in that bomb sent to the professor. They investigated me like you don't want to believe. Then they investigated Jimmy and Amy. Jimmy is a tinkerer. They took all his things. They took all the stuff the poor kid had. They had nothing to do with it. Jimmy and Amy were innocent [in] that case. I believed that from day one."

Bill Murphy believed quite the opposite, in fact. Whoever built the pipe bombs had to have some expertise in building explosives. And a grudge. The ATF knew that James Anderson and Amy Bishop had both. Murphy set out to prove it.

First he had to petition for a federal warrant to search cars, offices, and the Hollis Avenue home in Braintree where Amy Bishop lived with her husband. What they came away with made him even more convinced that at the very least Anderson was now a prime suspect. Proving Bishop knew anything about it would be more difficult, however. She had never been arrested, and when agents ran a "BOP," or a Board of Probation record on her, it came back clean. As far as they knew, the woman had never been in trouble before. She did not have a "CORI" or a Criminal Offender Record Information rap sheet in Massachusetts. There was no record of anything other than some minor motor vehicle violations.

Though the evidence certainly pointed to Anderson, getting the warrants had still been difficult. That changed when Proulx came forward. With his statements, Murphy and the postal inspector were able to obtain the search warrants they needed. Proulx had verified that Anderson had made a threat against his wife's boss. That man told agents that he was afraid of Amy Bishop. It took a while to convince the U.S. Attorney's Office they had a case, but with the cooperating witness it became a little easier. On April 13, 1994, the investigators got their warrant and searched the couple's home in Braintree, their vehicles, their places of work, and the elder Andersons' home in Foxboro. As a courtesy, federal authorities always tip off police brass in the city or town where they're conducting an investigation. So the Braintree police had been notified about the upcoming raid on the house. Not a single Braintree cop, however, mentioned to the federal agents that the place had been teeming with investigators, albeit briefly, on a December day in 1986, when Seth Bishop was shot dead in the Victorian house abutting the carriage house that Amy now occupied with her family. The ATF was already in the house when Braintree sent over a cruiser as a precaution. Not a single officer said, "Hey, remember the shooting of Seth Bishop at this address?" Sure, many cops had moved on by then. Retired. They had answered so many calls it could have been forgotten. It was unlikely, though. None of the Braintree cops wanted to have to answer questions about how *that* case had been handled. It was embarrassing.

Before collecting evidence at the locations named in the warrants, the agents again studied the bomb's materials and box. They didn't want to miss the smallest clue, a tiny detail that could lead to an arrest. The package had been sent fourth-class mail, with six twenty-nine-cent American flag stamps. The address for the Union of American Hebrew Congregations had covered up another New York City address, one for a company called Omega Publishers, located at 866 Third Avenue. Inside the package were the following:

- Four Sears DieHard 9-volt alkaline batteries with "2J" stamped on the underside of the batteries.
- Four snap connectors with blue and red wires.
- Two press-release roller-lever micro-switches.
- Two pipe bombs consisting of approximately 4 ½ inch length, nipple 1-inch diameter, end caps,

black coated multistrand wire with white insulation.

- The above batteries were held to the side of the packages by thick gauge wire.
- The pipe bombs were held to the side of the packages by thick gauge wire.
- The pipe bombs were held to the package by copper multistrand wire and an apparent cement/epoxy.
- Solder connected the wires.

The components were apparently assembled on a brown cardboard "nest" which was placed into the box and affixed to the sides of the box via the epoxy. But it was the box itself that provided the most important clue. The UPC, or uniform product code, which is used when an item is scanned and sold, had been torn from the box. But the agents were able to resurrect it at the postal lab, just as Murphy was able to lift the serial numbers from a weapon even if they had been defaced. It was the same sort of technology. The serial number of a gun was tattooed into its metal, just as a bar code can leave enough ink residue behind that its number could be read. The box had been sold by the company Avery Dennison, a corporation that made office supplies. The company was cooperative and was able to determine that it had shipped a box of Avery Dennison Analysis Pads, or five-column accounting tablets, in that particular box.

That is exactly what agents found on James Anderson's desk in his office at Harvard School of Public Health: a five-column accounting tablet. It was hardly a smoking gun. But it was nevertheless strange that a lab assistant at Harvard School of Public Health would have an accounting tablet used almost exclusively by accountants. And that was not all. Agents also recovered a receipt for a roller-lever micro-switch—exactly like the one that would have triggered the bomb sent to Paul Rosenberg. It was purchased at a Radio Shack in the South Shore Plaza in Braintree, the mall where Samuel Bishop had gone shopping the day his son, Seth, was shot dead by his daughter, Amy Bishop.

There were also receipts from a hardware store where someone had paid cash for end caps that could have been used in the construction of the casing. Because the purchase was made in cash, and the receipt was found in the couple's Braintree home, it could never be determined who bought the end caps. Computers were seized and searched. There was also a business card for an Alabama shop, Chalkville Bait and Tackle, specializing in "black powder pistols, rifles, shotguns, and supplies."

The evidence recovered alone wasn't enough to put the couple away, or even put them in front of a grand jury. The Feds remained convinced, however, that at the very least James Anderson was a principal suspect. What kept the focus on the couple was the fact that they were uncooperative, even belligerent, when agents attempted to interview them. They had immediately lawyered up, as cops say, and would not answer a single question. They were followed and photographed. Their lawyer was asked if the couple would consent to a polygraph test. They wouldn't, and the agents didn't have the authority to compel them to do it. They did have to submit to fingerprinting and were court-ordered to submit handwriting samples.

Murphy reached out to the ATF's Birmingham, Alabama, office and asked if there was an agent available to interview the owners of the Chalkville Bait and Tackle store. There was. That agent would question the owners and submit a report to the agents on the case. It did not go unnoticed that the store was not far from where the former Jimmy Anderson Jr. had grown up. In fact, by then, the elder Andersons were considering leaving Massachusetts for good to resettle in the south. They had not had much contact with their son until the investigation into the letter bombs began. When they did, Anderson Sr. told his son to haul ass to Alabama. His son didn't listen.

The Alabama ATF agent went to the store on May 9, 1994. Alabama is a long way from Massachusetts. It was as easy to buy guns and explosive powder in Birmingham as it was to buy micro-switches and end caps in the Bay State. The agent spread out photographs of Amy Bishop and James Anderson on the counter of Chalkville Bait and Tackle at 2457 Springville Road. There were six pictures in all. Each showed a different aspect of the suspects' faces.

"Any of these people look familiar to you?" the agent asked the owners, a married couple.

"No, sir."

"You have any records of selling black powder?"

"No, sir. We are not required to under local law."

The agent slid a photocopy of the store's business card toward the owners. "This belong to this store?"

"Yes, sir. But we haven't used those cards in more than a year-and-a-half," the owner replied.

"You have any employees that might recognize these two?" The agent tapped his index finger on the pictures of Bishop and Anderson.

"No, sir. I am the primary worker here. I'm here six days a week and I don't recognize them."

The agent asked to see the store's Acquisition and Disposition Book—which is required in any firearms supply location—to determine whether or not Anderson or Bishop had bought a gun at the store. They hadn't.

The gun that Donald Proulx said he purchased for James Anderson was never recovered during the execution of the search warrants. The agents were unable to locate the Ruger. Still, it nagged at them.

There were also some suspicious things found at Amy Bishop's office. Murphy and Mastrangelo had interviewed the department's secretary and asked to see the lab's printer. The laser-jet printing that Bishop used for her work "closely resembled the exterior address markings" on the package sent to Rosenberg, the ATF noted. Bishop also had a roll of 2-inch tape in her office, just like the tape used to seal the box sent to Rosenberg. The evidence was largely circumstantial, but that circumstantial evidence was becoming cumulative.

Murphy approached the United States Attorney's Office again. They had been working the case without rest for months. He wanted the evidence to be presented to a grand jury.

He got Assistant United States Attorney Theodore "Ted" Merritt, a controversial federal prosecutor who was hated by some law enforcement. He had a reputation for prosecuting cops with what they viewed as an unseemly degree of relish. But ATF agent Bill Murphy did not give a damn whether or not cops liked Ted Merritt. He was focused on making sure the letter bombers who tried to kill Dr. Paul Rosenberg would be found. Merritt was also an expert in public corruption. But at that time, he had no way of knowing that his role as a criminal prosecutor and as a public corruption attorney would merge with the Amy Bishop case. That would not come until later.

Merritt wanted to hear from Donald Proulx. The agents' cooperating witness suddenly clammed up. He got a lawyer and he wasn't talking anymore. Without his cooperation, Merritt refused to send the case to a grand jury. There were a lot of cases that were getting squashed in the U.S. Attorney's Office around that time. Those were ugly years for the Boston office of the FBI. It would later become apparent that FBI agent John Connolly had colluded with Boston gangsters. It was a quid pro quo arrangement. Connolly would feed information about rivals to the psychopathic head of the Irish mob, James "Whitey" Bulger. Whitey would throw the FBI a few high-profile arrests. When the relationship was revealed, witnesses had been murdered and John Connolly would be convicted of a litany of crimes, including conspiracy, which would send him to jail for the rest of his life.

The federal agents would not give up. Despite the mounting evidence against Amy Bishop, she continued to work at Harvard-affiliated labs and at Boston teaching hospitals. She was a very smart woman and a good scientist, even if she did have trouble getting along with her colleagues. The cops decided to approach Anderson while his wife was at work. They thought he might be more amenable to a discussion without his wife around.

Anderson was coming out of his parents' house with a cup of coffee in one hand and a pack of cigarettes in the other.

"Why haven't you returned my phone calls?" Murphy asked him.

"Ahhh . . ." Anderson stammered. "I've been real busy at work. I haven't had a chance."

Anderson didn't have anything else to say. He turned and rushed up the stairs toward the front door.

"You're going to have to talk to us," Murphy yelled at him. "You're going to have to show up in court at some point."

Anderson retreated into the house. Minutes later his

mother, Sandy, appeared at the door, according to Murphy's report.

"What's the matter?" she yelled. "What do you want?"

"We want to talk to your son."

Then they spotted the elder Anderson in the doorway. Jim Anderson Sr. recognized Murphy as the guy who had grilled his fellow Scout leader.

"When are you going to leave my boy alone?" Anderson yelled.

"I left a message last night for your son, sir. He didn't get it?" Murphy responded to the elder Anderson.

According to the report, Anderson responded, "You're a fuckin' bum."

With that, Murphy decided to leave. He wanted another crack at convincing Merritt to build a case against Anderson. Merritt agreed to a meeting with federal judge, Nancy Gertner, in the coming days to go over the evidence. There were the receipts from Radio Shack for the roller-lever switch. The strange five-columned accounting pad found at Anderson's office. The end cap receipts from Home Depot. Merritt remained unconvinced. Like most prosecutors, he only wanted to bring charges if he knew he could win. No one wants a loss on their record.

The U.S. Attorney's Office ultimately decided not to pursue any charges. The case was largely circumstantial, Merritt told the agents, and they just didn't have the evidence for a solid win. And with federal judge Nancy Gertner, the agents believed that prosecutors would need a slam-dunk case.

Moreover, Nancy Gertner was, frankly, being a pain in the ass. She was very liberal and loathed by police and prosecutors who saw her as someone who showed her bias for criminal defendants in many of her rulings. Her husband, John Reinstein, was the head of the

American Civil Liberties Union of Massachusetts. She was nominated to the bench in 1993—the same year Rosenberg was nearly killed by the letter bomb—by then-President Bill Clinton. It was not a surprise. One of her close friends at Yale just happened to be Hillary Rodham, who would later become Hillary Rodham Clinton. The women remained close.

The minute she was sworn in, Gertner immediately began to infuriate law-and-order types. She had represented Susan Saxe, a domestic terrorist with the Weather Underground who was charged with murdering a Boston police officer while a student at Brandeis University. Saxe was also charged with ripping off a National Guard Armory in Massachusetts and using the guns in the attempted bank heist that left Patrolman Walter Schroeder dead. (His brother would also die in the line of duty and Boston Police headquarters is named One Schroeder Plaza for the slain brothers.) She was criticized by prosecutors and legal scholars after she gave a black man who was a notorious gun-toting Boston crack dealer a reduced sentence because he was pulled over for motor vehicle violations more "than a white man." Citing the scourge of racial profiling, she gave him a downward departure on his federal sentence. The suspect was a known gang member with a long criminal rap sheet with drug and weapons charges. Prosecutors called foul, saying it was the ruling of an activist, not a federal judge. But that was Nancy Gertner. She had a tendency to side with defendants over the prosecution. The burden of proof rested on the government. Police felt that she made no attempts to hide it either. She frequently criticized the war on drugs and was seen as being lenient with drug dealers overall—even if they were gang members who ruled their drug cartels with murder.

There was one final meeting in May of 2001 before the case was officially put to bed. With a sense of dread, Murphy scrawled one last notation in the management log of his case. It read: "5-1-97. Meeting with Postal Inspector and USA Merritt." The next entry read: "5-25-01. Closed. No potential." Amy Bishop and James Anderson were never officially cleared in the case, but the government was required to return computers and other belongings seized in the raids. Discouraged and reaching retirement age, Murphy put in his papers and began to work as a consultant to the ATF.

Of course, in a matter of months, the entire Department of Justice, including the ATF, would focus most of its energies on another matter altogether: the terrorist attacks of September 11, 2001. With 2,996 Americans murdered, letter bombs mailed years earlier to a Harvard professor became a very low priority. The boxes of evidence in the case were sent to a federal storage facility.

By then Amy Bishop had also moved on. Allegations had swirled around her for months, but none of it seemed to affect her standing at Harvard University. She had landed another postdoctoral fellowship at the Harvard School of Public Health, investigating the role of nitric oxide and disease. Rosenberg remained afraid of her, and would later say so.

"There is something seriously wrong with that woman," Rosenberg told Bill Murphy. "She is dangerous." Of course, Rosenberg had no idea how right he was.

10

Sam and Judy Bishop finally decided to sell their sprawling Victorian home in 1996. They were getting older, it was too much house for them to handle, and they had been planning to leave for years anyway. The time was right. Amy, now freed from the federal investigation, seemed to have leveled out. She had three little girls, and while the Bishops hadn't really taken to her husband James, he was a good father. He took care of those kids while Amy was off advancing her scientific career.

For another thing, the place must have been thick with bad memories. There were the odd smears of discolored plaster that haphazardly covered the hole in Amy's bedroom wall. There was a splotchy patch job in the ceiling of the kitchen, too. There was the cheap new floor in the kitchen to replace the one that had been stained with Seth's blood. Even the wooden stairs that Amy had descended with the shotgun in her hands still creaked as they had that day. Sometimes, if Judy was in the kitchen, the sound of her husband's footsteps pressing down on the aging wood would startle her.

The Bishops had a buyer, a nice family who had been eyeing the beautiful home and its manicured landscape for years. Kelly Moore, the father, worked in the telecommunications business. His wife was Rochelle. The Bishops were not the type to have strangers traipsing through their home. So when the Bishops' family attorney, Bryan Stevens, whispered to Kelly Moore that the house was for sale, but would not be publicly placed on the market, he pounced. Stevens and Moore had been friends for years. They had talked about the Bishops and Moore made no secret that he and his wife had pined for their house for years, even knowing what happened there.

"We loved the house," Kelly Moore explained. "There was no way we weren't getting it."

Braintree is a small town of sorts, and people talked. Everyone knew that Seth had been killed in the kitchen, even if they also believed it had been an accident. The most popular story in circulation was that Amy had heard what she thought was an intruder and came downstairs with her dad's shotgun, which accidentally went off, killing her brother. There were rumors, of course, that Braintree Police Chief John Polio, certainly a controversial character, had pulled some strings to get Amy Bishop out of a jail cell that day. There was still persistent gossip that there had been something more than a friendship shared between Judy Bishop and Chief John Polio. Both Bishop and Polio strongly denied these rumors and there was nothing more than a professional relationship to tie them together publicly. There was also talk that Amy Bishop had always been intensely jealous of her little brother, that she had been unhappy that Seth was doing so well at Northeastern University, embarking on a career in electrical engineering, that he was overshadowing her own accomplishments. There were people in Braintree, including some police officers, who were convinced that Seth's shooting was no accident. *Judy Bishop had interfered with the investigation,* retired cops would lament over coffee at the downtown Dunkin' Donuts.

But Kelly Moore ignored all of the ugly chatter and chalked it up to gossip. Besides, even if it was true, he could hardly blame Judy for saving her daughter after she had just lost her son. "I would lie through my teeth for my kid, too," Moore said. He had always loved the grand Victorian from the outside. Now that he had seen the intricate wood carvings and the antique detail work he was not going to worry about what town busybodies said about the Bishops. He wanted to close.

He signed papers on the house in 1996 and moved his young family in. He and his wife, Rochelle, had two kids, a four-year-old son, Blake, and a one-year-old daughter, Abigail. Moore, however, did take note of one strange feature of the Bishop home that "gave him the creeps." Seth's room remained a shrine. Completely untouched since the day he died. There was a wood carving that spelled out his name over the bedroom door. His weight set was still in the corner, with barbells on the floor. His twin bed was unmade. The Revolutionary War wallpaper stood as a stark reminder of Seth Bishop's obsession with Braintree's historic place in American life. "It was like going back in time," Moore remembered. Before Blake would take that room over, Moore noted, the whole room would have to be emptied out and redone. He hoped the Bishops would be decent enough to take the dead teen's belongings out of the house. He wanted no part of that at all.

Judy was standing next to the Moores when they took the initial tour of the house. By then she had become thick, portly. The long, straight hair that she sported during her hippie days had turned from blonde to gray, but had not been cut in years. She was "earthy, crunchy," Moore would later describe her, with Birkenstock shoes and a face completely free of makeup. Moore only had a couple of encounters with Judy's husband, Sam. He knew that Sam Bishop was a Northeastern University faculty member who taught in the arts department. He found it odd, the extent to which the man played up the whole "nutty professor" look. He wore his beard long and tousled. His hair was mussed, as if intentionally. He barely spoke, aping the mannerisms of a "quiet, deep person," as Moore put it.

The closing on the house came in December of 1996, almost the ten-year anniversary to the day of Seth's slaying. Before it was made official, however, there was something the Bishops needed: Amy and James would get to stay in the carriage house.

The house was small, just 900 square feet. It was certainly cramped quarters for a scientist, her tinkerer husband, and their three children. The yard was strewn with toys from their three children. Not outdoor toys. Just toys. They were everywhere. The Bishops strolled over to the "dollhouse," as they called it, to introduce Moore to his new tenants. "The place was a wreck, an absolute wreck," Moore said later. "The husband was a quiet, happy-go-lucky guy. He wore his hair in a pony-tail. She was just weird. Intense. Sometimes she was all smiles and friendly. Sometimes she would walk right past us without acknowledging we were even there. It was not a good feeling to have them there."

But a deal was a deal. Plus, Kelly and Rochelle Moore felt bad for the Bishops. Sometimes Rochelle would catch herself staring at her son, and would get a flicker of panic in her belly at the thought of losing him. She knew that a young boy had died in the house where she was raising her own children. She was okay with that most of the time, unless that gnawing fear set in. Rochelle Moore didn't know how Judy had coped with something like that. They had to let Amy and James Anderson live in the house, paying $600 a month, from December of 1996 until the following April. It was then that Moore hiked the rent, mainly because he was tired of the clutter in front of the small house. He had also noticed that Seth Bishop's belongings had been moved from his old room—but were now being stored alongside Amy's belongings in the carriage house.

"I raised the rent from $600 to $900. I thought it might entice them to move," Moore remembered. He wasn't that pushy about it. He felt for the elder Bishops. In fact, he had forwarded stacks of mail to their new home in Ipswich. Among the junk mail, flyers, and leaflets were packages from a support group for grieving parents. Ten years later, it was clear the couple were still grappling with their son's death.

He approached James Anderson first, telling him he needed to raise the rent. The answer he got was surprising: "He told me I had to talk to his wife." For some reason, Moore dreaded the confrontation. He had seen Amy flip out over the smallest thing. He had watched her yell at her kids and had a feeling that she verbally lashed out at her husband in the same way. There was a lot of chaos in the carriage house at night. Frankly, Kelly Moore didn't want his kids exposed to it. He reconsidered even asking for the rent increase to avoid the encounter with Amy. Instead he reached out to Sam and Judy Bishop and told them that he needed to raise the rent. The Bishops in turn told Amy and her husband to move to Ipswich. Once again, Amy would be living with her parents. So would her entire family.

Kelly Moore's instincts about his tenant were not just vague misgivings about a woman with a past touched by violence. He was not the only one leery of the ornery scientist. Amy Bishop was once again working in a

Harvard-affiliated lab at Beth Israel Deaconess Hospital. Bishop began working at Beth Israel under a man by the name of Dr. Hugo Gonzalez-Serratos. Gonzalez-Serratos was on loan to Harvard from the University of Maryland, where he was a well-respected professor of physiology. He was sent to Boston to supervise a group of Harvard doctoral fellows, Amy Bishop among them, working on a grant-funded project to determine whether deficient cellular cyclic AMP concentrations may be responsible, at least in part, for striated muscle dysfunction, both cardiac and skeletal, in heart failure. In layman's terms, they were coming up with a drug doctors could prescribe to patients predisposed to heart trouble. Upon concluding their research, the fellows had to present a scientific paper to the head of the department, Dr. James Morgan, and to Dr. Gonzalez-Serratos. It was 1996. The paper was well written, Gonzalez-Serratos remembers, and was published in a New York medical journal. It read in part:

> These results suggest that therapy aimed at restoring cyclic AMP to normal levels may be effective with regard to improving systolic and diastolic function in the heart and may decrease the development of fatigue in skeletal muscle of patients with failure. The use of cyclic AMP-dependent drugs in clinical practice has been limited by side effects associated with raising total cellular content of this cyclic nucleotide. However, evidence suggesting that separate pools of cyclic AMP may exist within the cell raises the possibility that those pools associated with excitation/contraction coupling could serve as more specific therapeutic targets.

The results were exciting. If the scientists could tell doctors to control their patients' AMP, or adenosine monophosphate, a mononucleotide found in animal cells and reversibly convertible to ADP and ATP, heart failure could potentially be prevented. A physician might have a hard time explaining that to a panicky patient, but the research made sense to the medical community.

The small team working at the Beth Israel lab was ecstatic. That is until Dr. Amy Bishop saw where her name fell at the top of the paper. Instead of being the first author, considered more prestigious, she was named second, after another fellow named Dr. Jessica Grossman. Bishop was furious. She confronted Grossman, and launched into a volcanic tirade that Dr. Gonzalez-Serratos would never forget. According to American Medical Association manual of style guidelines for publishing medical research papers, "the first author has contributed the most to the work and the last author has completed the least." Amy Bishop did not like to be usurped by anyone. She didn't like it as a child when Seth got more attention than she did from her parents. She didn't like it at Harvard University where she was ignored by some of her academic peers. She didn't like it in Dr. Paul Rosenberg's lab where she had complained that he overlooked her important work. And she didn't like it now that Jessica Grossman was going to get more credit for their research than she was. It didn't matter that Grossman had worked on the project longer, or that she had spent considerably more of her own time on nights and weekends. Amy Bishop had "delusions of grandeur," Gonzalez-Serratos would remember, about her contributions in the laboratory. There was also something to be said for Grossman's ability to get along with her colleagues and to take criticism without falling apart. The same could not be said Bishop. That afternoon she began to wave a copy of the paper in Grossman's face in an aggressive manner. Other lab researchers stood, stunned, at what they were witnessing.

"I deserve to be first! Who do you think you are, you silly bitch?" Bishop screamed at her female colleague. "I did this work! This is my work. You are trying to steal from me." Grossman was so surprised by the tirade that she didn't respond. She was scared. She began to cry. Hearing the commotion in the lab, Gonzalez-Serratos and James Morgan, the chair of the Biology Department, rushed into the lab. Bishop was clearly out of control. The lazy eye that ordinarily remained half-closed was wide and fixed. It was a look they had not seen before. And frankly one of the doctors would remember it as frightening.

"What is going on here?" Gonzalez-Serratos asked.

"You are trying to ruin me!" screamed Bishop. "You are destroying my life! This is my work. I want to be first. This is unfair. I need to be first author! I need this! I need to advance my career!"

The doctors in the room were astonished. They had never seen a Harvard graduate, a scientist no less, behave in this manner. Bishop was hysterical. There was no way to calm her down. Her chest heaved with sobs, but her rage was frightening, particularly in the confines of a prestigious teaching hospital affiliated with Harvard University. It wasn't exactly a place where one expected to see a researcher explode into an expletive-riddled rage. Especially for a calm, kindly guy like Dr. Gonzalez-Serratos.

"The reaction was incredible," Gonzalez-Serratos remembered. "She broke down. She was extremely angry with all of us. She exploded into something that we never saw before in our careers. We tried to calm her down, but there was no calming her down. We told her first author was not as important as making sure we could continue the work and continue the grant. She would not listen. She kept screaming and swearing and crying. I will never forget it."

Already her professors at the lab thought Amy Bishop was problematic. Every time she was confronted with a problem in her research she would pout, or pick up her research and storm out of the lab yelling over her shoulder, "I'm going to talk to my husband about this. He knows more than most of you."

"It was strange," Gonzalez-Serratos said. "A Harvard fellow should say thank you for the advice and correct the theories. She would react with so much anger. Every time you had to talk to her you got a crazy reaction. She shared everything with her husband, who I never met. She would argue constantly that they were both smarter than everyone else in the lab. Unfortunately, that was not true. She thought she knew more than she did." Gonzalez-Serratos left to return to Maryland two weeks after Amy Bishop's attack.

James Morgan remembered the outburst, but also said he did not fire Amy Bishop on the spot because she "did some good work." Morgan, now a cardiologist at Carney Hospital in Dorchester, said Bishop worked in his laboratory at Beth Israel for a year after earning her Harvard doctorate. Of course, he was spared daily contact with Amy Bishop. He did not witness the whining and the complaining when others confronted her with her mistakes. "She did some good work when she was with me," Morgan told the *Boston Globe*. "She was a very smart, hard-working postdoctoral fellow who had a lot of potential." While she wasn't escorted out of the Beth Israel lab by security, which some thought should have been Morgan's immediate response to the outburst, her fellowship was not extended either. She would only spend a year on the team. That left her once again, albeit briefly, without a job or an income. Even if she wanted to pay the rent increase to her landlord, the family could not have pulled it off. She would be forced to move into a smaller apartment and beg her parents for cash. Again. It was humiliating.

When the U-Haul truck backed out of the driveway and away from the carriage house on his property, Kelly Moore heaved a sigh of relief. He felt bad for the elder Bishops, but there was something about their daughter that was unsettling. She even looked angry all the time, red-faced like a full bladder ready to burst. He and his wife looked over at the empty house the night the family vacated and went to bed happy. "At least that's over with," Rochelle would say.

Moore's old problem, however, was about to become the problem of Dr. Amy Bishop's new neighbors.

11

Amy Bishop liked to tell people that she was born in a cornfield in Iowa, because her mother had refused to go to a hospital. Sometimes she would even joke that her parents found her in that cornfield, that they picked her one night when the two stoned hippies were out partying in college. It was one of the stories that her neighbors in Ipswich, Massachusetts, picked up shortly after the Bishops arrived at 28 Birch Lane.

"If I were Judy and Sam Bishop," one resident on the block would tell an Ipswich police officer, "*I* would tell people I found her in a cornfield. I would never want to claim that woman as my own."

The entire Ipswich Police Department, every one of its members, would soon learn why Amy Bishop's Ipswich neighbors felt that way.

Amy and her husband moved into her parents' Ipswich home in 1999. After moving out of the Moores' house—formerly Amy's childhood home in Braintree—they struck out on their own at an apartment in Newton. That wouldn't last. Three kids. High rent. And James Anderson was consistently underemployed. His ventures as a self-employed computer engineering consultant were not bringing in enough money to pay rent and keep food on the table for the growing family. By now, Bishop had a permanent position as a postdoctoral fellow and research associate at the Harvard School of Public Health. She was investigating the role of nitric oxide in cell survival and disease after obtaining her Ph.D. in genetics at Harvard University. But her job depended on grants and her salary was paltry. It would be a long time before Dr. Amy Bishop would make the big bucks. Besides, the couple didn't like the bustle of a place like Newton. James Anderson had once called the Newton police to tell them an MBTA driver behaved belligerently toward him. A month later, Amy Bishop called 911 and told Newton cops that there was "a suspicious vehicle idling in front of her home." Neighbors often heard Bishop screaming at her husband and kids. Other times they would hear soothing violin music.

"She was a wacky one," neighbor Johnny Henk would say to other neighbors.

Besides, the couple wanted to have another baby. Sam and Judy Bishop loved their three granddaughters, but they told Amy over and over that she should keep trying for a boy. Plus, Sam Bishop had received a diagnosis of prostate cancer. The Bishops had always hoped for a grandson to carry on the legacy of the son they had lost and still kept framed photographs of in their home. Having James there to help out was a relief to Judy Bishop, and having her grandchildren around all the time gave her joy.

That said, there was nothing joyful about having Dr. Amy Bishop as a neighbor. Not a damn thing.

Birch Lane in Ipswich was one of those streets that young families sought out when looking for a first home or a place to raise kids. Basketball hoops were set up at the end of driveways. Big Wheels and bicycles were left on front lawns without a worry that they might go missing. Children played spontaneously on the street, which is secluded enough that there is never much traffic. The homes on Birch Lane were nice ones—ranging in price from $300,000 to $600,000—but there was nothing stuffy about the neighborhood. There were block parties and barbecues and shared birthdays. Mothers watched one another's kids. Everyone got along.

Except for Amy Bishop—who was known as the neighborhood "PITA," for "Pain in the Ass." She had a lazy eye, so it didn't take long for the mean children in the neighborhood to nickname her "Crazy Eyes." Neighbors thought her husband was no prize either. Sure, he had grown up in the South, but wearing cowboy boots and Colonel Sanders ties in a tony town in New England was sure to raise some eyebrows. And it did. His moniker on Birch Lane became "Captain Crazy Cluck."

Arthur Kerr was a tax attorney who lived next door to the Bishops. He would tell a *Globe* reporter that they were obnoxious from the start. "The first thing she told us was that she went to Harvard and how smart they were, and within days they had their first dispute with someone."

And if their strange attire and arrogant attitude were not enough to alienate people in their new neighborhood, Amy and James began issuing complaints about petty nuisances. It got so bad that the Bishops' next-door neighbor built a privacy fence. It was just one wall: a single length of fencing to separate their yard from the Bishops'. Amy once flagged down an ice cream truck driver and demanded he stop driving down Birch Lane. "My kids are lactose-intolerant," Bishop told him. "It's not fair that they have to see the ice cream truck." Astonishingly, the ice cream truck driver was so rattled by the encounter that he did stop selling treats on Birch Lane. Another time, she called the Ipswich Police because she couldn't reach her father. A patrolman conducted a well-being check and found out that Sam Bishop was there; he just didn't answer the phone when Amy called. "Didn't feel like talking to her," he explained to police.

Not long after, she reported her young daughters missing and insisted the cops file a missing persons report. The police did so, saying that Amy Bishop had told them that their daughters had left a friend's home without notifying their parents, which was out of the ordinary. "Normally phone calls are exchanged before children are allowed to leave someone's home and that did not happen," the cops noted on the missing persons report. Police officers walked out of the house with pictures of the girls, Thea and Phaedra, and started to ask neighbors if they had seen them. One neighbor said: "Yeah, they are over here playing with my kids. The Andersons knew that." The children were missing for about fifteen minutes all told.

A week after that report, James Anderson called the cops because a neighbor was using heavy equipment and "creating a disturbance." A cop arrived to find a home owner, Scott Lafoc, working on his own driveway with a roller to prepare it for new hot top. The officer noted that the "roller does not make much noise and the process has to be done for four hours." A few months later, James Anderson called the cops again because kids were making noise and smoking pot on the street. Police arrived and could not locate any kids. There was another 911 call placed about dirt bikes making too much noise. Once again, police arrived and there was no sign of the loud dirt bikes or the kids accused of riding them. There was still another complaint that there was "a band playing in the neighbor's driveway." Police instead discovered a teenager practicing his guitar in his family's garage.

Then came another complaint to the police about skateboarders riding their boards on Birch Lane at night. This one came from Amy. The cops had to sit her down and explain that children are allowed to ride bikes and skateboards on their own property. That wasn't enough. One day a teenager named Joey Lafoe, Scott's son, was riding his bike past the Bishop home. James Anderson shoved him to the ground. Joey went home and told his mom. She was not happy and rang the Bishops' doorbell.

"This is not happening. You will not put your hands on my kid," Pamela Lafoe, Joey's mom, said.

Amy Bishop slammed the door in her face. Then she called 911.

"This is going to come to blows," she told the responding officer. "This is nonstop. These kids are playing basketball and making noise [in the] front of the house."

Of course the police officer had to ask about the assault on Lafoe. Anderson denied it. The Lafoe family did not want to pursue charges because it would require additional confrontation with the Bishops. It went away. But it also started a war between the two families.

"Look, Mrs. Anderson," the patrol officer told her, according to a report. "Don't confront these kids yourself. Call the parents first and let them know that they are loud. Then call the police."

She would. Again and again. Less than a month later patrol cops were called to Birch Lane again. By now the couple were, as the cop put it, frequent flyers. "We could not do enough for this family," Ipswich Police Chief Paul Nikas would say. Every time a dispatcher's scratchy voice alerted them to a problem on the street, the officers would roll their eyes and sigh. Not again.

This time it was James Anderson calling to complain about the noise of kids playing outside. A frustrated police officer responded and found no noise. Minutes later he was sent back to the street, because another resident had called 911 to complain about James Anderson harassing them.

"This is Angel Hopping," she said. "James Anderson will not stop calling me. He keeps screaming 'Knock off the noise!' There is no noise. My kids are not making noise. It was me. A group of adults having a conversation on a back porch," she said.

Hopping was furious. For the twenty years she had lived there, neighbors often passed hot summer evenings on each other's balconies or terraces, having a few drinks and sharing a laugh or two. Oftentimes, they were laughing at the mad scientist and her kooky husband. Now, because of the pair, the kids had to run to another block to get an ice cream cone. They were afraid to play ball in the streets or ride their bikes. It was getting out of control.

"I want it on the record that I am sick of the Andersons' complaints and harassment," Hopping told the cops.

They couldn't blame her. They were tired of the Andersons' complaints, too. They were unrelenting.

James Anderson called 911 that same fall to complain that "the Hopping boy was playing his stereo too loudly." Once again, police arrived and didn't hear a thing. The officer and Angel Hopping commiserated for a minute about the "PITA," and the case was closed. Weeks after that complaint came another one aimed at the same family. For the same reason. Loud music. Police didn't even bother to show up. They called the Hopping household.

"Do me a favor," Nikas asked them. "Turn down the music." They did. Reluctantly. But continuing to engage with the crazies on Birch Lane was a losing battle.

The next 911 call came from Amy. She was griping about Pamela Lafoe. "These goddamn kids are driving up and down Rose Court and Birch Lane on their scooters and motor bikes. I can't take the noise. You told me I can't call the Lafoes so I am calling you."

The call was logged. No one was sent.

In 2001, neighbors noticed that Amy Bishop was getting even paunchier than she had been. After a few months it became clear that she was pregnant. Ordinarily, women on the street would organize a baby shower for someone who was expecting. They were all that tight-knit. But there was no way in hell they were going to do that for Amy Bishop. They were all just praying that the pregnancy would calm her down. That she would concentrate on her three kids, soon to be four, and leave them alone. And she did. The last 911 call was placed in July of 2001. Amy's son, who would indeed be named Seth after the brother that she had shot dead, was born a month later. Finally, the Bishops had a grandson. Finally, the Bishops had a namesake for the son they had lost on a winter day in 1986.

Things were quiet for the Ipswich Police. It would be a short reprieve. That would not be the case, however, for the Peabody Police.

It was not completely out of the ordinary for the Peabody Police to be called to the local International House of Pancakes for a disturbance. Usually, however, those calls came at night, when drunks would occasionally beef with one another in the restaurant. But it was not even noon on March 16, 2002 when Peabody police officer David Murphy was called to the IHOP for a fight.

He arrived and found a woman who said her name was Michelle Gjika crying. Her two children were also crying. With one hand she held her toddler boy's hand and with the other she nursed a welt on her head.

"I don't know what happened," she told the policeman. "I was sitting with my kids and this lady come over to me and says, 'You bitch. Give me that booster seat. I was here first.' I told her that my son was in it and she punched me. She was screaming, 'I am Doctor Amy Bishop! I am Doctor Amy Bishop!' She was absolutely crazy."

The account of the fight was verified by a restaurant manager. The place was packed. It was a busy restaurant most days, but Saturday mornings were sheer chaos. Gjika was seated in a booth by a waitress who then brought her over a booster seat for her little boy. Bishop and her family—including James—were seated in a nearby booth. Amy waved over the waitress and said, "Hey. We are going to need a booster seat."

The waitress apologized and explained that it would be a short wait. She had just given another woman the last one.

"But we were here first," Bishop yelled. "Who the fuck do you people think you are? We were here first." Her husband James sat in the booth wordlessly. As usual. He knew enough by now not to interfere when Amy was embroiled in an argument. He knew no one could win when his wife was fired up—including him.

"Please. Watch your language. There are kids around," Michelle Gjika asked.

"Shut up, you dumb bitch. You have no idea who you are dealing with," Bishop responded. The argument had become so loud that forks had stopped scraping against plates. The roar that came with a packed pancake house on a Saturday morning was gone. It was silent as patrons stared at the two women.

This was too much for the manager, Dagoberto Sandoral. It was a family restaurant. He was not going to have F-bombs flying around the restaurant from this weirdo and her ponytailed husband. The manager approached Bishop.

"Ma'am, you are creating a disturbance. I am going to have to ask you to leave."

But Bishop wasn't going anywhere. She was flabbergasted that she was not getting her way and that a lowly pancake house manager had questioned her authority. Once again she screamed, "I am Doctor Amy Bishop!" Then she went over to the victim and punched her on the right side of the head. The woman was so startled she began to cry. Her kids wailed.

Of course, baby Seth was crying. Bishop's three daughters were upset. James was silent. A patron called 911 to report the attack. Bishop grabbed the kids and snapped, "Let's go!" at her husband. The clan stormed out of the restaurant. Her daughters had seen their mother behave like this before and went outside without any pushback. The woman who had been punched ran outside to get the license plate number of her attacker. Bishop was putting her kids inside a red 1988 Ford Taurus. She turned and saw Gjika scribble her plate number on a restaurant napkin and yelled the refrain that she had repeated so many times during the altercation:

"I am Doctor Amy Bishop."

Gjika went back inside to wait for the police. Officer Murphy told her to try and calm down while he interviewed the manager. He was clearly flustered.

"She was acting like a crazy person," Sandoral told police. "She was swearing at the other lady and yelling at the lady's kids." The waitress was also horrified by what she had witnessed: A grown woman punching a mom in the head? "It was insane. She kept swearing at everyone and screaming. Her husband wasn't doing anything to calm her down at all," she told the cop.

Murphy ran the plate that was provided by witnesses to the attack. He found the car was registered to Amy Bishop-Anderson of Ipswich. Her number was listed and he gave her a call from the station when he returned.

"Ms. Bishop. I am calling about an incident at the IHOP in Peabody."

Bishop launched into a five-minute tirade about how she was the victim. She claimed that Gjika had shoved her. "I was afraid of her. She attacked me."

It was going to be a long day, the Peabody cop knew. He informed Bishop that she would be receiving a criminal summons to appear in court.

"Are you kidding me?" Bishop replied. "I want to take a complaint out against her." She was within her rights to claim that she was a victim. Murphy knew all too well that the witness statements pointed to Bishop as the aggressor.

Murphy sighed. "Ma'am. The court is open on Monday morning. You can swear out a complaint there."

Surprisingly, Amy Bishop—who had a lot to lose with her new Harvard job—did just that. She swore out a complaint against Gjika before going to work. She scrawled it in handwriting—but refused to put her address on the "civilian signed complaint form," writing: "I would like to keep address confidential as the defendant and her husband seem vituperous." Yes. Vituperous. As in "worthy of blame." Once again, she had to alert the court that they were not dealing with a big-mouthed housewife in a spat over a booster seat. She was a scientist who viewed her opponent as "vituperous."

On the form there was a place to list witnesses that

could back up Amy Bishop's version of the incident. She scrawled: "James E. Anderson. No other witnesses would see past James Anderson, myself, or the individual as it was in close quarters." Of course, the woman who had been punched in the side of the head had the restaurant manager, the waitress, and other patrons verify her story.

When asked to describe the facts Bishop wrote:

1) The defendant initiated an argument. 2) She appeared angry and agitated toward her children before she initiated the argument. 3) She swore at me and my husband and we decided to leave the restaurant. 4) She blocked our exit and grabbed my shirt at the waist and announced, 'I swear to God I am going to knock you out cold.' As the defendant raised her hand to claw my face I blocked her and shoved her back. 5) We left the restaurant and she followed us.

Bishop also filled out a victim impact statement provided by the Essex County District Attorney's Office. "There is an emotional impact on my children who were present and witnessed the event."

There was even a spot where Bishop could recommend a punishment. "The case against the defendant should *not be* dismissed. The defendant arrived agitated and abusive toward her children and then initiated an argument with me and my husband." She signed the victim impact statement with two large *A*s, as in Amy Anderson. She was going to use her married name on this one. She probably would not want it to get back to anyone at Harvard that she had been embroiled in a donnybrook with another mom at the IHOP.

Besides, by then Amy Bishop fancied herself a writer, an aspiring novelist. She had joined the Hamilton Writers Group on the North Shore. Her writing would be flowery even on a police report.

Bishop was summonsed to court by Peabody Police on charges of disorderly conduct and assault and battery. The Essex County prosecutor handling the case, Cesar Archilla, noted something in Amy Bishop's demeanor that gave him pause. She was an angry woman. And she was a mother. She had kids. It was disturbing to think that a mom could become angry enough to punch a stranger in front of her own children. He recommended that Amy Bishop be forced to attend anger management classes. The judge, Santo Ruma, did not heed the prosecution's recommendation at sentencing. Instead, the case was continued without a finding, which means Amy had to admit to the facts of the case as stated by the prosecution, which she did. Then if she stayed out of trouble for six months the plea would not go on her record and the charges would be dismissed. She was ordered not to have any contact with Gjika and she was released.

She would have no criminal record and she would avoid a jail cell. Again. There would not be any anger management therapy for Amy Bishop, even though a seasoned prosecutor recognized that she needed it.

The case could have blown up her career and put her academic future in jeopardy. She punched a woman in the head over a booster seat in a packed pancake restaurant. That doesn't exactly bolster one's resume.

One would think that Amy would do well to lay low and avoid any contact with police, but that wasn't the case. She still pursued charges against the woman she punched in the head, claiming assault. The poor woman was dragged into court and forced to hire a defense attorney. Not only had she been attacked at breakfast with her kids, it was going to cost her money to defend herself from accusations leveled at her by the nutjob. Gjika's attorney, Stephen Scalli, remembered Amy Bishop and her husband well from when he had to take a deposition from them in the case.

"She was clearly the dominant one. Her husband shuffled behind her in his cowboy boots with this string tie on, like Colonel Sanders, and did everything she told him to do. I could not believe she was making my client's life miserable . . . until I met her. She was clearly not right in the head. They were very odd people."

Bishop's lawyer asked Scalli to cut a deal where both women faced a judge and admitted assaulting one another so both could have the charges dropped. Scalli refused. That would involve Michelle Gjika having to tell a court that she initiated, or participated, in the brawl. No way.

"My client was punched in the face in front of her kids. She didn't do anything wrong. I'm taking it to trial," he said. The trial didn't last long. Scalli was successful in having the charges against his client dismissed. By then, Amy Bishop had already been given the lenient sentence imposed by the judge.

With the pancake house matter disposed of, Amy Bishop resumed her frequent contact with the Ipswich Police Department. The next 911 call placed to Ipswich Police was stranger than any that had come before it. Amy called police in March of 2002 to report that she had gotten a "prank phone call" from a guy in the nearby city of Peabody who claimed that he "had a one-night stand with someone named Amy Bishop, who he met in a bar." Apparently, that woman had had a child named Joshua. The caller had apparently found an Amy Bishop in the phone book and called to ask her if she was the woman he had knocked up. He was demanding to see his son. Amy insisted to the caller that she had

The Bishops' house in 1986. *Photo by Gary Higgins,* Patriot Ledger

A Band-Aid can covers the hole in Amy Bishop's bedroom wall after she fired a shotgun blast.

From the library of Michele McPhee

The *National Enquirer* story found on the floor of Amy Bishop's room.

From the library of Michele McPhee

Shotgun shells recovered on Amy Bishop's bed where she told police she was loading her father's weapon.

From the library of Michele McPhee

The back door of the Bishops' home where Amy Bishop fled after her brother was shot dead. *From the library of Michele McPhee*

Desperate attempts to save Seth Bishop's life were evidenced on the blood-spattered kitchen floor.

From the library of Michele McPhee

Braintree Police Chief Paul Frazier on right.

Photo by Braintree PD

Jay Sullivan of the Braintree Police interviewed Amy Bishop the night she shot her younger brother Seth Bishop dead.

Photo by Braintree PD

Former Braintree Police Chief John Polio in 2010.

Photo by Gary Higgins,
Patriot Ledger

David Traub of the Norfolk County District Attorney's office with Bill Keating the night Keating became a Congressman, replacing Bill Delahunt. *Photo courtesy of David Traub*

Chief Paul Nikas of the Ipswich Police. The police responded to frequent calls from the Bishop home when the couple lived on the North Shore of Boston.

Photo by Scott Goodwin Photography

Retired Braintree police officer Tim Murphy talks about the shooting death of Seth Bishop and the inquest into the victim's sister, Amy Bishop, who is now charged with his murder.

Photo by Greg Derr, Patriot Ledger

US Representative William Delahunt announces his retirement weeks after the UAH shooting at the hands of Amy Bishop.

Photo by Alex Jones,
Patriot Ledger

Former auto worker Tom Pettigrew talks about Amy Bishop holding him at gunpoint in 1986 at an inquest into her brother's murder.
Photo by Greg Derr, Patriot Ledger

Massachusetts State Trooper
Detective Captain William
Christiansen leaves court car-
rying a shotgun case.
Photo by Greg Derr,
Patriot Ledger

ATF agent Bill Murphy at a crime scene in 1986, the year he investigated a mail bomb sent to the home of Harvard professor and Children's Hospital researcher Dr. Rosenberg.

Photo courtesy of Bill Murphy

Dr. Paul Rosenberg was nearly killed by a letter bomb sent to his Massachusetts home. Amy Bishop and her husband were the prime suspects in the attack.

Photo by Harriet Rosenberg

not been to any bars; had never had a one-night stand in her life; and he had the wrong Bishop. He wouldn't listen and kept calling. Amy Bishop called Ipswich Police.

"The guy started asking me about my sex life," Amy told Nikas. "He knew what I looked like. He described me. Maybe he is watching me. How does he know what I look like? I don't have a son named Joshua. My son's name is Seth."

Amy Bishop denied an affair to police. She said she didn't recognize the name of the man calling her claiming to be the father of her love child. The scientist sat at her computer and started to conduct some research. She came up with an address and even a phone number for the name the man gave her.

As a precaution, Nikas called the Peabody Police to see if they had a guy by that name who may have been "known to cops." By now, everyone knew that Amy Bishop was a big deal at Harvard. And she had a big mouth. The department did not want to take any chances that there really could have been a stalker after the scientist. The name she gave police was real. So was the address. And the guy had a history of violence, including an arrest for an assault on his girlfriend. He also had a couple of drunk-driving raps and an old drug offense. Ipswich Police brass knew it was a good idea to keep an eye on this case. Bishop's position at Harvard warranted the extra attention even if everyone at the station knew she had some issues.

He reached out to the Andersons and got James.

"Yeah. We got another call tonight. The guy sounded drunk. He was asking for my wife," James Anderson told the cop. Nikas set out to find this Sean guy and put an end to the calls. He left a message with a friend saying: "If you see Sean, tell him to stop calling the woman in Ipswich. If he doesn't, I'll lock him up."

He left that message at every number he had for Sean. Which wasn't easy. The guy clearly had a booze problem. When he wasn't couch hopping he lived in a hotel. Finally "Sean" called the officer back. He swore he didn't remember calling any Amy in Ipswich. He promised it wouldn't happen again. Then Nikas called Amy Bishop.

"I think these calls arc going to stop."

For once, Amy Bishop uttered a phrase that the Ipswich Police had not heard up until then. "Thank you. I am very happy with this outcome."

That didn't mean that the 911 calls would stop, however. The Lafoe kids would keep riding their motorized dirt bikes. The Andersons would bitch about it. There would be a block party with a hundred people and the Andersons were the only ones left out. In fact, Amy Bishop was so despised that one day she came out of her house to find that someone had let all the air out of her tires. Strangely, that was the one time she didn't call the cops.

12

"I have a Ph.D. from Harvard University," the woman said, standing up at a school committee meeting in Ipswich.

But then, the other parents in the room knew quite well that Amy Bishop was a Harvard graduate. "God, that woman mentions it every other sentence. Harvard Harvard Harvard," said Lenny Cavallaro, the parent of a teenager a year younger than one of Bishop's daughters, to another parent. "I have never heard this woman talk for very long without mentioning Harvard." The other parent nodded. Agreed. Bishop was not only well known to the police in the town; she was also well known to teachers and school administrators. She was apparently an expert not only in her field, but in matters of school administration and parenting—of both her own kids and everyone else's.

Bishop was making an impassioned plea to change the curriculum at Ipswich Middle School. Today, she was standing against block scheduling, in which the school scheduled double periods of some subjects— like English and music—for the first half of the year, and other subjects—math or science—for the remainder of the year. Some of the other parents agreed with her, and among them was musician, writer, and then-literary agent Lenny Cavallaro. Sure, the woman could be abrasive, but she was clearly very bright and passionate about her children. After Bishop finished her plea, Cavallaro followed to express his own misgivings about the plan. They were ultimately unsuccessful, but after the School Committee meeting they struck up a conversation that would burgeon into a friendship, and then eventually into a collaboration.

"We got friendly. Our daughters were roughly the same age. She seemed pretty level-headed," Cavallaro said.

Cavallaro had always nurtured literary ambitions. Amy Bishop told him—as she told most people she met—that the National Book Award–winning novelist John Irving was her second cousin on her mother's side. Irving was the author of acclaimed novels that were then revised for the big screen including *Cider House Rules*, *Hotel New Hampshire*, *A Prayer for Owen Meany*, and *The World According to Garp*. Bishop used her blood ties to the Vermont writer to engage in a constant stream of braggadocio. She talked about "my cousin John Irving" a lot. She thought the relationship could open some doors for her in the publishing world. Cavallaro agreed, at first. Sometimes those relationships could get a literary agent to listen. They started to talk about writing. Bishop was obsessed with the poet Sylvia Plath. Like Amy, Plath had been born and raised in Massachusetts and suffered with depression.

Amy had been at it for a while already. Years earlier, she had become an active member of the Hamilton Writers Group, which mingled published authors and scriptwriters with amateurs. Amy always introduced herself to new members of the Hamilton Writers Group the same way. "Hi. I'm Dr. Amy Bishop. I work at Harvard.

My cousin is John Irving." Frankly, some of the writers there found it annoying, especially the ones whose work had been critiqued by Bishop. They found her commentary caustic, even mean-spirited sometimes, and the whole Irving thing had become tiresome. When she started it, some of the veterans of the writers group exchanged glances with one another and rolled their eyes. *We know already. We know.* Still, she showed some talent and she showed up. They accepted her as an oddball and left it at that. Of course, no one really knew about Amy Bishop's past, about the dead brother or the letter bomb investigation or the gunpoint standoff with police when she was twenty-one years old, so when they urged her to *write what you know*, that adage so many writers relied on, no one knew that her life could read as a murder mystery or as an episode of *CSI: Braintree*.

She had joined the group shortly after moving back in with her parents seeking feedback for the three novels that she had written, along with short stories. Each of her fiction books, however, seemed to expose a side of Bishop's real personality. Her two latest novels were based on the life of a scientist who was charged with the mission of saving the world. Her first was told through the eyes of a 12-year-old girl in Belfast and was called *Martians in Belfast*. She went as far as copyrighting that book. It made sense that she believed in extraterrestrials. One of the altercations she had with neighbors in Ipswich involved a weird accusation that Amy had pointed a bizarre futuristic fake weapon at neighborhood kids who rode past her house on Birch Lane on their dirt bikes. Despite the copyright, the novel never went anywhere. She kept trying. For a busy woman, she was prolific in the writers' group. She turned in short stories and draft novels and read the work of others in the group, critiquing with a red pen. Hamilton Writers

Group was founded by a medical writer named Rob Dinsmoor who also wrote comedy scripts for cable networks MTV and Nickelodeon. Dinsmoor described Bishop's work for the group as science fiction and described the woman as very strong-willed.

Dinsmoor and Amy Bishop became friends and she shared with him repeatedly that she was hoping that her writing could get her out of the stuffy environment of academia. She wanted her work to catapult her into a realm where she could be respected not only for her research, but for her writing. "She had a terrific creative streak," Dinsmoor would tell reporters. "She was always very good at writing about violence." What Dinsmoor may not have realized is that Amy Bishop's work was not entirely fictional. In one novel, which was disseminated among the group and was later posted online by a blogger at interestingni.blogspot.com, there were eerie parallels to Amy's own life.

It was called *Jerkville*. Bishop named the lead character Andrea Bissop. She was a scientist who was conducting vital research that was being dismissed outright by the "jerks" in her life. In an excerpt from one chapter posted by a blogger on the Internet, there were strange parallels to the scientist's own life. She wrote about a violent encounter at a Macy's department store that sounded strangely like the incident at the IHOP. The chapter also contained a startling sentence about racking the slide of a gun—just as she had in Braintree as a young adult right before she shot her brother Seth dead: "Frustrated, Andrea pulled out a Glock .40 from her oversized handbag, racked the slide, and double-tapped the surprised clerk. With a pair of vertical holes in her forehead, the clerk crumbled to the floor like a dropped napkin."

There was also a line about two young patrol cops

jumping out of a cruiser with their guns drawn. Just as Braintree cops Ron Solimini and Brian Murphy had done the day she shot Seth. She even compared Dr. Andrea Bissop to Ted Kaczynski, the Unabomber: "She does important scientific work, sorta like Ted Kaczynski." It also had a line about teaching a "boss at a lab" a "valuable lesson about performance reviews." Just like Dr. Paul Rosenberg.

The book would not be published and Bishop did not bother to file a copyright for it as she had with her first novel. If talent was not going to get her published, relentless ambition might. She craved fame and attention in the worst way and had told Dinsmoor, "My dream is to quit academia and write fiction full time," She wanted to be a female Michael Crichton, the famed medical thriller writer. That's where Lenny Cavallaro came in. He was a respected musician, a published author. He had credibility in the publishing world. He had even sold a few books as an agent and continued to collect royalties from those authors' works. Throughout their blossoming friendship, the two writers talked about collaboration. That venture would come after Cavallaro had spotted a piece by columnist Nicholas Kristof in *The New York Times* about cow DNA and its connection to anthrax and disease. He forwarded the piece to Amy Bishop with an e-mail, writing: "I think there is a literary angle here. It strikes me as fascinating. I was thinking Neanderthal DNA. We've got this disease breaking out killing people and we create a new species using Neanderthal DNA."

Amy was ecstatic. She loved the idea.

"I'm in," she responded, Cavallaro said. "This is my field. I already have two novels working but I will drop everything and work on this one. I want to bring James into this."

Cavallaro did not have a problem with James joining the project. He had become friendly with him during visits at the Ipswich house. He found him to be pleasant enough, if a little henpecked. He was a smart guy and knew his stuff scientifically. It could work with three minds coming together to create an outline for the book. They decided to call it *Amazon Fever.* In fact, James Anderson came up with the title. He would also contribute a great deal of the writing. Most of the writers' meetings took place at the Bishops' house on Birch Lane. Cavallaro was going through a cantankerous divorce and he was emotionally strained. The meetings about the book were cathartic. The work got his mind off the chaos at home. It also solidified his friendship with Amy and her husband.

"I spent a lot of time there, especially with my marriage falling apart. I saw the fights with the neighbors, but I also saw Amy's side in those matters. She had a cranky baby she was trying to get to bed and there was loud noise or loud bikes. She had some legitimate points," Cavallaro remembered.

The first draft of the working novel developed a heroine who was a researcher who needed to come up with a cure for a disease that spelled doom for civilization. Bishop, Anderson, and Cavallaro wrote about ninety pages together and Cavallaro was pleased. It had the potential to be a medical thriller that would translate to the big screen. He also knew that Amy was beginning to consider a move, and that she was in talks with the University of Alabama at Huntsville. In late 2002, she began to press Cavallaro to shop the manuscript "on spec" hoping that a publisher would see its potential and give the writers an advance. But Cavallaro knew the business. He cautioned her that publishers were not going to give unpublished writers an advance on a spec novel. It didn't happen. But Amy was insistent.

"Tell them I am a Harvard Ph.D. Do they know who the fuck I am? This fucking book has bestseller written all over it," she screeched. "Jesus Christ, Lenny. You have no balls at all. You have two scientists helping you with this project. Your job is to be an agent and sell the fucking thing."

Cavallaro was stunned. Bishop went from a mom trying to put her kid to sleep to a raging lunatic in a matter of seconds. "She became very foulmouthed," Cavallaro said. "She was screaming and swearing. She wanted it to go to an agent. She again told me, 'I have a Ph.D. from Harvard. Did you know that?' Well of course I knew it. The whole town knew it."

Cavallaro tried to be sympathetic. Maybe the outburst was provoked by exhaustion. The job. The kids. The husband. The noisy neighbors. He had not seen her rage like that before and wrote it off as an aberration. They had about ninety pages of *Amazon Fever* written. It was about a researcher named Olivia who was trying to save the world from a global pandemic that left women unable to bear children. The character embarks on a trip to the Amazon to study how the disease is killing monkeys. In the draft, Olivia has a fling with an Asian doctor in the lab and is struggling with depression. The character is also obsessed with her career and how heading off the pandemic would make a lasting impact on her future. Olivia questions her marriage to her husband, Steve. Amy Bishop did name another character after her husband, though. "James Anderson" is a crack genetic sequencer at UAH. Harvard University is mentioned numerous times, with one sentence reading: "At Harvard, even the bartenders were snobby."

"She was here to save her career," Bishop wrote in the novel, "which was flagging in perpetual postdoctoral fellowship." The novel also contains a passage where the character wonders if her husband regrets their marriage. Olivia starts to think that Steve felt she had "tricked him into thinking she was a healthy person."

"'Steve, I had no idea that one day I would get depressed or that one day I would have a severe allergy attack,'" she wrote. "Steve looked up from eating and asked, 'What?' Olivia looked into Steve's eyes and saw that they were flat, unreadable, more inscrutable than ever."

There were even references to old family problems in the novel. "'At some point,'" says Olivia, "'you can't hide behind your past to recuse yourself from being a human being.'" Cavallaro realized that the character Olivia closely mirrored Amy Bishop's professional life. He had no idea how much of the writing had been taken from her real personal experience. In *Amazon Fever*, Olivia had killed her brother; her mission to save the world is undertaken in his honor. She wants to make amends to him by becoming a great scientist. In order to do that, she needs to get a tenured position at a good university.

There is also a moment in the book where Olivia is listening to a talk radio show that gives out its phone number repeatedly. The number in the manuscript is, in real life, the Harvard Medical School's confidential Research Compliance Hotline.

There is also a passage where Olivia dreams. "She knew she was a professor, having finally achieved tenure. Her huge family sat at the table; her mother, father, her sister, Steve's parents and the children—her many children. . . . She felt warm, happy, fulfilled, and yet she knew it was just a dream."

"I knew nothing whatsoever about her brother. I knew nothing about the allegations at Harvard with the attempted bombing," Cavallaro said. "Who knows what kind of fantasies Amy was having."

He started to have reservations about the book. He had lost control of the writing. Amy and James had taken over. He didn't even know if he wanted his name on it as an author anymore.

"The writing was terrible. The plot was awful. Her heroine had become Amy Bishop. She tried to make a person that was *almost* as great and wonderful as Amy Bishop."

But, to make his friend happy, Lenny Cavallaro contacted an old friend in Los Angeles who worked at a well-respected literary agency. He talked up his collaboration with Bishop and truthfully indicated that both Amy and her husband had great scientific minds and could come up with a thriller concept that could translate to the big screen. He asked his pal for a favor. Would he be willing to talk to Amy Bishop on the phone and give her some direction? The agent agreed. It didn't make Bishop happy, though. Nothing could.

"These fuckers don't know who I am. Lenny, you're an agent. You start shopping it around," she screamed into the phone. "We need to get some money for this so we can keep going."

Cavallaro tried to calm her down and explain that no one gets an advance for a work in progress, except maybe her second cousin John Irving. Maybe, he suggested, she could call him for the advance. He was being sarcastic, but Amy flipped out.

"This is my novel. I don't need a creep like you to represent me," he remembers her saying. "I don't want you to represent me. I don't want you to write it with me."

He sucked in a breath. A part of him was grateful that the conversation was happening over the phone. It was so irrational, so irate, that he was unnerved. He remembers feeling panicky.

"She was very shrill. She was screaming like a child. 'Mine. Mine. Mine. Mine.' She wouldn't stop. Everything was another flavor of bullshit with Amy."

With that, the friendship ended. So did the collaboration. Amy moved to Huntsville, Alabama—with the manuscript on which Cavallaro had spent so much of his own time collaborating. They exchanged e-mails about *Amazon Fever.* Amy told him "she would swear on a stack of Bibles that it was hers, hers, hers. I was stunned it turned out the way that it did."

The friendship ended badly. After the family's move, the Andersons would return to Ipswich to spend summers with Amy's parents. Cavallaro got his hands on an updated version of *Amazon Fever* and said that it was unreadable.

"The mechanics of her prose are abysmal. For a woman with a Ph.D. even in the sciences she was really inarticulate. She couldn't spell cat without a K. Working with her was excruciatingly painful. She was very thin-skinned. She flew off the handle constantly."

Of course, Lenny Cavallaro was not the first person to make that observation about Bishop. And he had no way of knowing that her obsession with obtaining a tenured position at a university—which she referred to constantly in their book—was very real indeed.

The last report filed about the Bishops by the Ipswich Police Department would come on April 27, 2003. More kids behaving menacingly on their bicycles. It was ignored, but there was gossip on the block that the Bishops were at it again. Then came the news that made neighbors exuberant. Dr. Amy Bishop had landed a position teaching as an associate professor of biology, a tenure-track position, at the University of Alabama in Huntsville. This is what she had worked so hard for. Tenure. Lifetime job security. James could be closer to his family. Amy would not miss her neighbors, but she would miss her writers' group in Hamilton.

They began to pack up their belongings. The residents of Birch Lane would fondly remember the day that family left. The kids weren't so bad. By then they had four: the girls, Lily, Thea, and Phaedra, and Amy's dead brother's namesake, Seth. As the U-Haul carrying their belongings pulled away, neighbors came out of their house and began to cheer, fists pumping in the air, laughing.

One of the Hopping kids yelled out, "Ding Dong, the witch is dead!"

Within minutes, everyone was singing that chorus from *The Wizard of Oz*. The Lafoes suggested they have a pizza party to celebrate.

"Those poor people in Alabama," Pamela Lafoe laughed.

She had no idea how right she was.

13

Tell a Northerner you're moving to Huntsville, Alabama, and the response will likely be, "Uh . . . why?" Especially those New Englanders who tend to think that Boston's nickname, "the Hub of the Universe," is well deserved (even though it was coined ironically to poke fun at Brahmin hauteur). After all, Massachusetts is the birthplace of freedom. Boston was the city where Paul Revere took off on that famous ride, and it was the heart of the resistance against the British. Four United States Presidents were born in Massachusetts, including George H. Bush, who lived on Adams Street in Milton—a street named after John Adams and his son John Quincy Adams, the second and sixth presidents. Of course, most people know the Kennedy Dynasty originated in the state. The best universities in the country—Harvard, of course, and MIT—train the future superpowers of the world.

But Amy Bishop was a scientist. She knew that the real Hub in her profession was quickly becoming Huntsville, Alabama. Biotech and genetics were a burgeoning industry in the college town and she could be a big fish in a small pond. Huntsville had earned the nickname "Rocket City" because it has been on the forefront of space exploration since a German scientist named Dr. Wernher von Braun relocated to Huntsville. When John F. Kennedy made the space program a pivotal part of his administration, the city thrived. Today it is the home of the Marshall Space Flight Center, which has provided NASA with thirty-two Saturn rockets, including six used to land astronauts on the moon. The people of Huntsville were proud to be considered ground zero for the Apollo program, and at one time it was believed that one in thirteen Huntsville residents worked in engineering. The United States Army Aviation and Missile Life Cycle Management Command is headquartered there at the Redstone Arsenal, where chemicals and munitions were manufactured during World War II.

Huntsville was and is a city of very smart people, where a family could pick up a decent house for less than $150,000 and a gorgeous one for under $250,000. In Boston, those prices couldn't get you a decent studio apartment in a condominium building. Amy Bishop and her family could live well here. They wouldn't have to depend on her parents anymore. James could conduct more of his own research, do more consulting. They would be *appreciated*. In her novels, Amy Bishop repeatedly bemoaned the lack of respect her work and her position commanded. She hated the fact that she was a nobody, and her character Olivia in *Amazon Fever* would refer to herself as "a nobody" more than once. In Huntsville, she was part of the intellectual elite, without the snobbery of Harvard types. She would finally fit in.

It's also a beautiful city. Relaxing. There are botanical gardens and sprawling green space. When *Forbes* magazine came out with a list of the 25 best places in America to retire in 2010, Huntsville came in eighth. A year earlier, the same magazine named Huntsville as one of the top five cities for recession recovery. In fact, financial journalists from prestigious outlets like *The Wall Street Journal*, *BusinessWeek*, and *CNN* repeatedly referred to the city as ideal for people looking for jobs in the defense, engineering, or technology fields. But it wasn't the gardens or the golf or the history that made Huntsville so appealing to Amy Bishop. It was not the proximity to James's parents, who had moved to Prattville, Alabama, in 1992. The Andersons did occasionally visit their sons on the South Shore of Massachusetts, but for the most part they were grateful to be back in the real south. But now the elder Andersons lived only about an hour and a half away, so the kids could get to know their paternal grandparents. It was not the fact that Amy had finally landed a tenure-track position at a prestigious university. She loved the city because she had heard over and over that there were more engineers and Ph.D.'s in Huntsville than anywhere else in the world. Not in the country. In the world. At least three hundred companies had invested in research at the area's universities.

Dr. Amy Bishop had finally arrived. After all the false starts and laboratory fights, she was finally in a city where minds like hers were tapped to do great things. She was in a breeding ground for brilliant work. She could make her mark. She could "make amends to her brother" as she had described in her novel, by "being a great scientist." Her job only paid $66,000 a year, but it was not about the money. It was about the grants she could win, the medical papers she could publish. Plus, while that wasn't a livable wage for a sole-providing mother of four in Massachusetts, the money went a lot further in Huntsville. The University of Alabama at Huntsville was a small school. It was not a first-tier institution, but it was striving for the same respectability that Bishop had been seeking. It would be a good match. She was an older professor in her first tenure-track job. In a university magazine, *Science Horizons*, the chair of the Biological Sciences program, Gopi Podila, heralded Bishop's hire. In it, he was quoted as saying that the arrival of "the neurobiologist from Harvard University" would help bring a "new dimension to our department's research and teaching potential."

The school administrators were happy to have a scientist with Harvard credibility. So happy, in fact, that they never bothered to fully research her résumé. On it, Bishop had claimed that she worked in a lab run by the vaunted researcher Bruce Temple for three years, when it had only been one. She also exaggerated her experience at Beth Israel Deaconess Hospital, where she had feuded with Dr. Hugo Gonzalez-Serratos. Her fellowship lasted less than a year and was not renewed. She claimed on her résumé that she worked there from 2002 to 2003, which technically was true but was misleading to the university. She did not list professors that she had worked with on her résumé as contacts.

The Bishop family—James, Amy, Lily, Thea, Phaedra, and Seth—moved into a subdivision in a suburb just southeast of Huntsville in 2003. It was a big change from the Victorian-era homes of Bishop's childhood, or the quaint, shingled houses that lined Birch Lane in Ipswich. McDowling Drive was in one of those newish neighborhoods, developed in the 1970s, where identical homes were built on identical plots. The couple had paid $190,000 in cash for the house. It was a Garrison Colonial that Jim and Sandy Anderson had scouted for them. They loved it. It had a swimming pool, an in-law apartment, and a carport. There were five bedrooms and a manicured lawn with old, magnificent trees that had been saved when the land was cleared to make room for the subdivision. It was the first home they had owned and lived in without family or close neighbors, like the Moores had been when Amy lived in the carriage house next to her childhood home after it had been sold.

Amy Bishop's new home was as far from the University of Alabama as her childhood home had been from Boston. She had never minded commuting, then or now. The drive gave her a little bit of quiet time, without kids clamoring for her attention. She had driven from Braintree into Boston for years, then from the North Shore into Boston. The ride from McDowling Drive into the university took about twenty-three minutes, leaving her over three-quarters of an hour a day to be alone with her thoughts. She had retired FBI clerks and other law enforcement types as neighbors. There were no issues. No 911 calls. The neighbors rarely saw the couple.

"Amy loved raising her kids here," James Anderson would later say. "This was like a dream house to her." Anderson began a business venture he called Cherokee Labsystems, and listed their home address at 2103 McDowling Drive as the company's address. The business was run out of the small in-law apartment in the back of the house. The company's motto was "Cherokee Labs . . . Exploring the Laboratory of Life." On the company's website he described his services this way:

Cherokee Labsystems utilizes a background of scientific, engineering, and practical know-how to deliver solutions to corporations and academic researchers. Prototyping and Proof of Concept: We specialize in the 'What if?' of scientific research. Give us your idea (sticky notes are okay) and we will work with you to determine its feasibility. If not, we will work together to find out how to make it work. Laboratory Design:

Science advances faster than buildings can be renovated. As scientists and contractors, we know how to work with design engineers to construct an efficient laboratory. Instrument service: We stand behind our solutions. If we install it—we service it.

The kids flourished in Huntsville as well. Lily was able to attend the University of Alabama at Huntsville for free, one of the perks her mother earned as a UAH professor. Lily had been surrounded by science her entire life. She began to study genetics, and was attending classes taught by her mother's colleagues in the biology department. Her sisters Thea and Phaedra attended Lee High School. Both of them excelled academically and musically. Phaedra was also a gifted writer and would earn a creative writing award. Seth could walk to his elementary school, but his dad usually drove him. After all, James Anderson ran his company from home. "We're a family of geeks," Anderson would say with pride. "My kids have been studying science since they were old enough to read. We bring them to music lessons and after-school stuff."

The family had dinner together as often as they could. It was important to Amy that they maintain that. Over the dinner table they would talk about school and politics. Amy had always been a staunch liberal Democrat. At Harvard she had been a member of MoveOn.org—an activist group that swung far to the left. Alabama was far more conservative than Massachusetts had been. James's parents voted Republican, which in Amy's eyes made them borderline evil. She wanted to make sure her kids were brought up morally, and to her that meant they had to understand that the Democrats were the only party that mattered. That was how Sam and Judy Bishop had raised their children. That's how Amy would raise hers.

They settled into a life that was centered on family. There were not a lot of outsiders invited to McDowling Drive. James's parents did not see their grandchildren as often as they would have liked. Everyone was busy. The kids had school. James had the company. Amy had her students and her research. They didn't need friends. They had one another.

So, for the first time in her life, Dr. Amy Bishop felt a sense of ease and comfort. It still was not enough. It was as if her happiness made her even more insecure than usual, gave her a sense of impending doom that her newfound serenity would somehow be snatched away from her. She knew that her husband kept a gun in the house. He always had. That's one of the reasons why the ATF had targeted them for investigation after the letter bombs were sent to Rosenberg. One night, Amy turned to her husband and told him that she wanted to go to the shooting range and learn how to fire his handgun. James didn't think very much about it. He had grown up around guns. His father was the Scoutmaster and had taught the boys a lot about antique weapons. James told Amy he would take her shooting at a nearby gun club. He still had that pistol that his buddy had bought for him in New Hampshire, skirting the tough weapons laws that were in place in Massachusetts.

James Anderson had never really learned what had happened to Seth Bishop. He had been told Amy's brother's death was an accident, but the circumstances were never, ever discussed among the Bishops. He had always thought to himself that Seth took his own life, and he couldn't blame the Bishops for not wanting to revisit or discuss something so extraordinarily painful. He had never asked Amy what happened that December day in 1986 and she never offered up the information. In Alabama, having your wife one day announce a newfound interest in joining a gun club was not all that extraordinary. He didn't give it much thought.

"It's probably not a bad idea to be prepared for anything," James Anderson told his wife about honing her handgun skills. "Maybe it's a good thing to be able to protect yourself.

"You hear about all these university shootings . . ."

14

However settled she felt in her new life in Alabama, when classes began, Amy Bishop started having problems with some of her students almost immediately. She wouldn't make eye contact. It was like the students made her nervous. Especially the female nursing students. They found her aloof and arrogant and would complain on the popular website ratemyprofessors.com that she brought her politics into the classroom. Sometimes the topics would veer off from genetics and go into the liberal agenda that was so often discussed at Harvard. In fact, one of her students would go as far as to write on the website:

"Neuroscience essentially turns into a bioethics class. She's a liberal from 'Hahvahd' and let's [sic] you know exactly how she feels about particular subjects," wrote one student. "Dr. Bishop is very unclear in her test preparation, grading, and overall teaching style. She is not at all organized and neither are her lab instructors. The tests are fairly easy and you never really have to go to class except on review day." Another student wrote: "Sci-fi to quantum mechanics with a little art history thrown in the mix." A female student noted: "For a Harvard graduate, she had very little common sense."

Her class evaluations were mixed. Some students

found her style motivational, but others said she was difficult to follow and would give tests full of surprise material that was not in the assigned reading or related to her lectures. Others still found her lectures lackluster, said she read straight from the textbook and didn't offer up enough help. Bishop's relationship with some of her students became so strained at one point that a group of coeds signed a petition to have her removed from the classroom. That move was extraordinary. To have students loathe a professor strongly enough to collect signatures, which these students did, shows that Amy Bishop was not just difficult to follow or dull. She was making life miserable for her students. The students went as far as to hand-deliver the petition to Dr. Podila, who had months earlier put out a press statement praising Bishop's arrival.

The school administrators dismissed the students' petition. They chalked up the complaints to the first-year jitters of a new professor. Perhaps the students were not prepared for a challenging class offered by a Harvard-educated neurobiologist. Besides, teaching was only part of her job description. She was also expected to conduct research that would help the school earn grant money from private donors and federal funding. Grant cash was the name of the game and school officials felt confident that Dr. Bishop could rake some in with her background and lab results.

Of course, there were some people who had a problem with the types of experiments Bishop conducted. Many felt squeamish at the idea of severing the spines of live animals to determine whether neuron recovery could be induced by subjecting the paralyzed animals to varying doses of nitric oxide. But it was Bishop's abiding passion. If her work was successful, she could help people struggling with multiple sclerosis or ALS.

That was the subject of Amy Bishop's research plan—which would be published on the University of Alabama's website. In 2003 she wrote:

The overall goal of my laboratory will be to explore resistance to nitro-oxidative stress in CNS cells. The specific aims are to:

1) Determine if the adaptive resistance extends to other oxidants and other CNS cell types.

2) Determine which cellular targets of NO-medicated damage are protected by HO1 induction and induced adaptive resistance.

3) Characterize NO-medicated increase of HO1 mRNA stability and/or transcriptional induction of HO1.

4) Determine what other genes are turned off by HO1 induction and whether their induction/inhibition is necessary for the induced adaptive resistance.

5) Characterize the role of HO-1, HO-1 mediated heme metabolism and iron in induced adaptive research.

6) Characterize the role of HO-1, HO-1 mediated heme metabolism and iron in induced adaptive resistance.

7) Characterize the role of cytostasis and differentiation in NO resistance.

8) Eventually use whole animals for studies of induced adaptive resistance in the CNS.

9) Whole animal studies of induced recovery from spinal transection.

10) Study the influence of low gravity/high radiation environment of space flight on resistance mechanisms to oxidative stress in CNS.

Clearly Amy Bishop did not have any moral issues surrounding experimenting on live animals, which is necessary when exploring genetics and trying to find cures for diseases.

In 2006, Bishop had some success, and the university heralded her for it. An internal publication announced that Dr. Amy Bishop had developed the InQ, a new, sealed, self-contained petri dish. Her version was described as reducing many of the problems with cultivating tissues in the fragile environment of the petri dish. It enabled researchers to test drug interactions and other effects on human cells in a sealed environment so there would not be contaminants or other particles that could cause unwanted interactions. It was a huge success and would bring in more than a million dollars in funding for the university. Bishop's invention would come to be marketed by Prodigy Biosystems, which raised $1.2 million in capital financing from a company called Biz-Tech.

Bishop's colleagues were thrilled. These kinds of innovations brought more than money to UAH; they brought credibility and respect. UAH would own the patent for the InQ and take fifteen percent off the top of all income earned with its sale. Then UAH would hand over seventy percent of their cut to the researcher. Bishop could stand to make a lot of money. It had been predicted that the invention could earn a net revenue of $25 million annually by 2014. The InQ was projected to go on sale in the summer of 2010; the dishes were slated to sell for $30,000 apiece. It was a long time coming, but Amy Bishop was finally receiving the praise she so desperately craved.

"This remarkable technology, which will change the way biological and medical research is conducted, was developed by Dr. Amy Bishop, an associate professor in the Department of Biological Sciences," the university's president, David B. Williams, wrote on his blog.

(It was called Dave's Blog, and every professor on campus wanted to be mentioned in it.)

What Dave's Blog did not mention, however, is that Bishop's husband, James Anderson, had a great deal to do with the invention. The couple had applied for a patent for the petri dish in 2006. The invention would secure Anderson a full-time job at Prodigy—his first in years. His wife was a member of the company's board but not in a paid position. UAH was quick to recognize their paid researcher, their associate professor. But those administrators were not so quick to acknowledge that she had had a lot of help from her husband.

In January of 2009, Bishop was featured on the cover of *The Huntsville R&D Report* with a story titled: "Prodigy Biosystems' nifty device will rock the cell growth world." The magazine focused on Alabama's engineering, space, and genetics community. To be featured on the cover was a coup for a scientist, especially one desperately seeking tenure after six years as an associate professor. The magazine's science writer, Anna Thibodeux, was almost giddy in her coverage of the Prodigy's invention, writing: "A Huntsville start-up company's innovative new cell growth machine promises to cut the costs, size and maintenance involved in the mechanics of cell generation and it's about to hit prime time. When the first device—dubbed InQ—rolls off the production line this summer, its inventors believe it's going to replace the petri dish, its more than 130-year-old predecessor, in laboratory experimentation and advancing biotechnology." Inside the magazine was a photo spread of Amy Bishop, UAH coinventor and company CEO Aaron Hammons, Vice President of Product Development Micah Harvey, and BizTech CEO Dick Reeves, who was financing the project. James Anderson did not pose in the photo. His wife looked happy. She was smiling, which was a rare thing to see when Amy was photographed.

The story went on: "Hammons is the CEO of Prodigy Biosystems, the company formed to develop and market the device, and he says his first impression [of the invention] was, 'Why hadn't someone done this before?'

"InQ coinventor Amy Bishop credits the coming together of a group of people with certain skills and crossover knowledge in a series of highly fortunate events fueled by Huntsville's evolving entrepreneurial spirit."

The story then quotes Bishop as saying: "It's great to actually see it hit the market, and the sooner the better. My colleagues think it will change the face of tissue culture. It will allow us, as researchers, to not live in the lab and control our tissue culture conditions, including the sensitive cultures including those like adult stem cells. The conditions to differentiate those have to be exact, and the incubator will help that."

The writer explained the formation of the idea: "tired of applying 1920s science to the rapidly advancing work of biotechnology, [Bishop] approached her husband, Jim Anderson, chief science officer of Cherokee Labsystems in Huntsville, about inventing a portable cell incubator. Together, she and Anderson designed a sealed, self-contained cell incubation system that is mobile and eliminates many of the problems with cultivating tissues in the fragile environment of the petri dish. It also has an onboard computer that maintains and regulates the incubator, allowing tighter control of the cell environment."

The gushing about the married couple's invention in the magazine went on for seven pages. It ended with a quote from Dick Reeves: "You have to create the right kind of environment for this to work, and you have to bring together the right kinds of people," he said.

"Huntsville has always had many of this kind of person, comfortable with uncertainty and with incomplete information, willing to push the established envelope in order to accomplish something new. Doctor Amy Bishop and her husband, Jim, inventors of InQ, are this sort of person. They are difficult people for many of us to deal with because they are unwilling to accept the established way of things, and they believe that better is possible."

Reeves was certainly right about one thing. Dr. Amy Bishop and her husband were difficult for many people to deal with. But he was dead wrong about how comfortable his new business partners were about uncertainty and incomplete information. Bishop, in fact, hated uncertainty, and when that magazine hit the stands she was obsessed with one thing: obtaining tenure.

For someone who was so obsessed with tenure, though, Bishop seemed to care little for publishing her work. In the publish-or-perish world of academia, this was a serious problem. Bishop published an annual article in 2004, 2005 and of course 2006, but then there wasn't a word published for three years. There was no explanation at all for the lull. It was certainly going to be used against her. Amy complained that publishing was a "cookie-cutter approach to science." Her bosses did not share her sentiment.

Feeling the pressure, in 2009 she began to write again. Bishop had secured a $220,000 grant from the National Institutes of Health that led to a paper published in the peer-reviewed *Journal of Neurochemistry*. That journal would publish another Amy Bishop–authored paper that same year.

Two good papers. Two papers that would garner her credit in a respectable publication that was taken seriously by other scientists. But it would be the third paper she authored in 2009 that should have raised an eyebrow. It was titled: "Effects of selective serotonin reuptake inhibitors on motor neuron survival." The papers list as authors: "Anderson L. B., Anderson P. B., Anderson T. B., Bishop A., Anderson J." and was printed in the *International Journal of General Medicine*. The journal was considered a vanity press.

Apparently, no one at the school thought it odd that the paper was written by four people named Anderson. If they had checked, they would have figured out quickly that the four of the supposed authors' initials happened to match the names of Bishop's husband and three daughters: Lily B. Anderson, Phaedra B. Anderson, Thea B. Anderson, and James Anderson. The paper listed James Anderson and their kids as employees of Cherokee Labsystems in Huntsville: her husband's company. Most professors in Bishop's position published far more research papers, and in peer-reviewed journals. Falling behind and increasingly desperate to bolster her chances at tenure, she tried to pass off research conducted in her home with her family, and published in a vanity press. In other words, she cheated.

By then, Bishop was lobbying full-time for tenure. She had begun the process of submitting the university's prepared application package detailing her teaching, research, publishing, institutional, and even community accomplishments. At UAH, once you worked for five years in the associate professor program, there was a five-step process toward achieving tenure. It began with a departmental review and then it was turned over to a college-level tenure committee review. From there it went to a university-level review board, and, finally, the provost. If a tenure-track professor is not granted tenure after six years, however, the university will no longer employ them. The clock was ticking.

It would be a long, agonizing year waiting to hear if she got it. "She was consumed with tenure," her husband would say. "She deserved it. She earned it." A month before the tenure list was made public, Bishop penned a press release about a science experiment conducted in her family's backyard. It was picked up by a UAH student newspaper, *The Exponent*, and ran under the headline: "UAH Launches Space Experiment." It read:

> At exactly 8:07am on Saturday, March 7, a two-month-long project was successfully off the ground and into the air. The Colleges of Science, Nursing, and Engineering all worked together to launch a balloon that carried a payload of nerve cells into space, measuring how they are affected by radiation in the atmosphere. A couple dozen students and spectators watched the enormous 2kg balloon as it made its journey above the atmosphere.
>
> Organizing three different colleges to collaborate on one project is no small feat, but the success of this experiment proves it can be done. "It's hard to get biologists and engineers to work together!" remarked case manager Alwin Heuer. The College of Nursing funded the project, the MAE Department's Space Hardware Club constructed the balloon assembly, and Amy Bishop of the biology lab provided the nerve cells.
>
> A unique aspect of this project includes the payload itself. Before this experiment, there was no way to transport living cells in a portable environment. James Anderson, owner of Cherokee Lab Systems and creator of the cell drive transporter, combined all his knowledge of electrical and computer engineering and biology to invent the device. "It wasn't easy to create, and I've been working on it for a while, and this experiment gave me a reason to finish it." The device is patent-pending.

After the balloon was set loose, a team of chasers immediately jumped into their vehicles to pursue the balloon via a GPS tracking system. It reached a height of 99,000 feet (18.75 miles), and eventually parachuted down northeast of Chattanooga. Everything was intact on recovery, and the cell drive transporter performed its job perfectly. When taken back to the lab, many of the cells were dead, and the next step is to grow the living ones and see how they react.

"We love working with MAE guys, and we couldn't have done this without them!" says Nursing Professor Lynx McClellan after the payload was recovered. "Now we're excited to work with the Biology Department to study the cells."

Ultimately, though, Bishop's self-promotional efforts fell flat. In April of 2009, she received word that her tenure had been denied. She was apoplectic. And she was not going to take no for an answer. She filed an appeal—and a complaint. There had been a male colleague—whose name was never released by the university—who complained out loud that Amy Bishop "was crazy" and that she should not get tenure. The comment was repeated back to Bishop and she filed a complaint with the Equal Employment Opportunity Commission claiming gender discrimination in the denial of her tenure. That professor spoke, on the condition of anonymity, to the *Chronicle of Higher Education*. The woman made him nervous and he didn't want to be on the record as being the one who said she was crazy. He confirmed that he had called Bishop crazy and did not regret it. He also said he was pressured by university officials to withdraw the remark after she filed the EEOC complaint, but that he refused, saying that he knew something was wrong with Bishop "five minutes" after he met her. He was a member of the tenure-review committee and had voted against her. "I said she was crazy multiple times, and I stand by that," the unnamed professor told the *Chronicle*. "The woman had a pattern of erratic behavior. She did things that were not normal."

After the denial, Bishop began to beg colleagues at the university for help. Dr. Debra Moriarty, dean of the graduate school, thought Amy was her friend. That friendship became strained when Bishop began to push her to help lobby to reverse the decision. It was the same story with another psychology professor who had joined UAH with Bishop in 2003. His name was Eric Seemann and he would recall how Bishop "seethed" with rage when he ran into her the last day of the spring semester. The tenure list had been released. Seemann's name was on the list. Bishop's was not. "These people are against me!" Bishop screeched at him. She would continue to rant almost incoherently. She sounded paranoid. "This tenure process is slanted. They want to take me down." Seemann later recalled the encounter in interviews with reporters.

"There are people in my department who have a personal beef with me. These people are directly involved with the tenure. I got a raw deal," Bishop continued.

Seemann listened politely, he said, but did not interject. He had heard it all before. He had been at a meeting with Bishop and other colleagues where she was, again, complaining about the tenure process. She rambled. She went as far as to say:

"I am arrogant. I am aloof. And I am superior in my attitude. But that doesn't mean I don't want to get along with people," Seemann remembered her saying. It wasn't the first time Bishop would be described as arrogant, even if it was Amy Bishop herself who was brazen enough to say it out loud when describing herself. She told another faculty member in her department that she was "better than him." It was easy to provoke Bishop, get her going. Some of her colleagues would do just that and then recount the "crazy Amy" stories over drinks after work.

Seemann never reacted to Bishop's tirades. There would be many. Some professors knew that Bishop was a brilliant researcher, but she had a reputation for being difficult, hard to get along with. He said, "I learned a while back that arguing with Amy was a one-way street."

Bishop hired a lawyer to fight the tenure decision. She kept a thick file documenting the tenure fight on her family's kitchen table. "I'm not going to be the one driving a bus," she complained to her husband repeatedly. "There is no fucking way I am going to be driving a bus."

She was referring to the sad case of Dr. Douglas Prasher. The former Woods Hole, Massachusetts, oceanographic biology professor was a brilliant molecular chemist who had to abandon his research in 1994 when his funding dried up. He landed a job at a NASA subcontractor's lab in Huntsville, but lost that job after funding cuts. Prasher was forced to take a job driving the courtesy van for a Huntsville Toyota dealership, earning ten bucks an hour, to make ends meet. Meanwhile, his colleagues went on to the win the Nobel Prize in chemistry in 2008, based on his research, but he was not included in the win because only three scientists could be named. Still, he was gracious and congratulated his former colleagues. "I am happy for them," Prasher said. He was invited to the Nobel awards ceremony and attended them with his wife. It was a story that Bishop repeated over and over again.

Bishop knew Prasher's work and was horrified at his circumstances. "They fuck you and then they steal your work," she complained to her husband and anyone else who would listen.

When students became irate at University President David Williams about a new policy requiring freshmen and sophomores to live on campus—which they claimed would cost too much and affect diversity—Bishop joined them in calling for his censure. The students were upset, saying the plan was too expensive and would affect diversity. Amy was happy to get on board. She would have done anything to get back at the school. She badmouthed Williams and his idea in the *Huntsville Times*. "It will generate a different economic strata and diversity," Bishop said. She wanted it to stay a commuter college, which would make it more affordable.

Then, on a Friday in February, Amy Bishop received an e-mail from the university. Her husband called it a "nastygram." She had exhausted her appeals, the letter read. As of May, Dr. Amy Bishop would no longer be employed by the University of Alabama at Huntsville. She would have to pack up her lab at the end of the semester.

It was over as far as school officials were concerned.

Amy Bishop saw it differently.

15

It was Friday, February 12, 2010.

Dr. Amy Bishop's first class began at 10:20 a.m. It was Anatomy and Physiology. Her students did not notice anything strange, well, stranger than usual about their professor other than she seemed a little distant and distracted.

Her next class, Introduction to Neuroscience, began at 11:30 a.m. It was Bishop's favorite. The twenty-two students she taught in that class liked her enough to send a petition, signed by all of them, to try and save their professor's job. It had been delivered to her department head and began with: "Dr. Bishop is a brilliant and excellent instructor. She is very responsive to the students."

The petition was started by C. Rena Webb, a Huntsville attorney who was studying biology so she could work in patent law. Webb had really liked Bishop's class. She found the professor, "very sweet, very open," if a little insecure. And that insecurity made her endearing. Here was a brilliant woman who was unsure of herself. It made Webb like her even more.

Webb was in the front row of the Neuroscience class that morning. She had expected Bishop to thank her for the petition. But Dr. Bishop seemed distracted. She had a strange look on her face. She announced that she would cut the class short. Then she didn't. It ran its full course. Bishop stared straight at Webb, which was odd. Every student knew that Bishop struggled with making eye contact. Not that day.

"She made continuous eye contact with me the entire time we were in there," Webb would say later. "I felt so uncomfortable. I kept looking up at the projector."

Bishop began to stammer. Her students remembered snippets of the discussion. Evolution. Chickens. Dormant genetic programming. Coding of dinosaur DNA. It was a jumble, they would tell the *Huntsville Times*. Unexpressed genes. Evolutionary triggers.

"I'm going home," Bishop suddenly announced. "I'll be back this afternoon to finish up a grant proposal."

Webb looked from the projector to a table at the front of the classroom. Bishop never carried a purse, or a briefcase, or even a backpack to class. Not ever. But on that day she dropped a canvas bag on the table. There was a weird shape in the bag. It was eight inches long and shaped like a cylinder, Webb would remember. Bishop caught Webb staring and shuffled the bag around so the item wasn't as noticeable. She kept her eyes locked on her student.

"I thought, Well, what would you be hiding in a bag? Why would you have to hide the shape of something,'" Webb told *Dateline NBC* producer Sarah Karlson. "She just moved it so you couldn't see the outline of it anymore. She didn't look at it again."

The class ended at 12:25 p.m. Bishop drove back home and had lunch with her husband. James Anderson did not remember anything odd about his wife's demeanor. She asked for a ride back to campus so she could attend a faculty meeting. There was nothing strange about that. Prodigy's offices were not far from the campus, so they commuted together a lot. Besides, it was Friday night. Date night. It was part of their routine to leave the older girls home with Seth, who was then eight, and go off on their own for a coffee or dinner.

"She didn't say anything peculiar," Anderson said. "She said she was going to put her time in. Get in. Get out. Just a run-of-the-mill faculty meeting. I'd pick her up and we'd go out."

The meeting was held on the third floor of the Shelby building. It was scheduled to go over routine matters. The fall schedules. Budgets. Mundane subjects that faculty members from the biology department had to discuss before going home for the weekend. There were thirteen people crammed in the room around an oval table. Before the meeting, students who volunteered in the department carried in extra chairs. Bishop took a seat at the corner of the large table near the door.

It was 3:57 p.m. Biology Department Chair Gopi Podila was about to wrap up the meeting. He had voted in favor of giving Bishop tenure and had given her a reassuring smile when she sat down. Podila's support of Bishop from he time she was hired and during her tenure push remained unwavering. It would not save his life. Everyone in the department knew Bishop was upset and some even tried to comfort her. Bishop had the canvas bag cradled in her lap.

According to reports, Dr. Debra Moriarty had her head bent over her notes when the sound of gunfire ripped through the room. Moriarty's head snapped up. She saw Bishop with her hands wrapped around the handle of a 9-millimeter Ruger handgun she had pulled from the bag. A woman, Dr. Maria Ragland Davis, had been shot in the head. Davis would be the first to die.

Bishop kept moving.

The bullets kept coming.

Dr. Adriel Johnson had been sitting next to Davis. It happened so fast, he didn't have time to move from his seat. Bishop shot him in the head. Then Bishop twisted to her right and fired a shot square into Podila's chest as he tried to back up away from her. The body count was now three. Davis, Podila, and Johnson were dead.

The rampage was not over.

Bishop made her way down the row, "shooting her targets in the head," eyewitness Dr. Joseph Ng would describe.

Dr. Luis Cruz-Vera was shot in the chest. Staff assistant Stephanie Monticciolo was shot in the face. Dr. Joseph Leahy was hit in the head.

Bishop had started with the faculty member closest to her and went down the row, splattering blood and brain matter over the conference room.

Dr. Ng threw himself to the floor. So did five of his colleagues who were sitting on his side of the table. Dr. Moriarty would later describe crawling under the table for cover. Instead of trying to get away and hide, Moriarty said she grabbed at Bishop's ankle. At first she whispered to herself, "Stop it. Stop it." Moriarty had been Bishop's friend. The women had eaten lunch together. Their friendship had deteriorated with Bishop's unrelenting obsession with tenure and her harassment of Moriarty, but there had been a bond. Moriarty was hoping that bond would save her life.

Bishop snapped her leg and shook off Moriarty's grip. Then she turned to the woman and pulled the trigger. Moriarty heard a thunderous click. Then another. Then another. The gun was empty. Moriarty pleaded with the woman she had worked with for six years, the woman with whom she had discussed child rearing and traded photographs of each other's children. In fact, the whole department was tight-knit. They had hosted dinner parties at one another's homes. Bishop had sat at their dining room tables. Moriarty had even talked to Bishop about writing a grant proposal together after she found a new job.

Moriarty tried to engage the mom in Bishop, begged her to stop.

"Amy, don't do this! Think about my grandson. Think about my daughter! Don't do this! Don't do this! Amy! Please! You know I've helped you. I'll help you again. It's me, it's me."

Moriarty crawled toward the door. Bishop followed her. As she paused and pulled an ammunition clip out of the canvas bag and began to reload, her colleagues pounced. "We rushed her. We pushed her [into] the hallway and closed the door," Ng wrote to a friend in an e-mail that was published in a California newspaper. "We barricaded the door and called 911."

Moriarty locked the door. Dr. Robert Lawton and Dr. John Shriver dragged a small coffee table to the door and propped it up so bullets could not be fired in from the other side. Then the men grabbed a small fridge to stack in front of the table.

Dr. Luis Cruz-Vera was the first to whip out his cell phone. He was bleeding from the chest wound. "I think I'm hit. I have to hand the phone off."

A 911 dispatcher coached Moriarty as she held pressure on her wounded colleague's bullet hole. There was no exit wound, so the bullet was lodged somewhere in his body. Two survivors pressed napkins to Leahy's head. Ng pulled off his shirt to stop Monticciolo's bleeding.

"At the time I saw two dead bodies already and several wounded," Ng would later describe to his friend. His e-mail mentioned nothing of his own attempt to save the severely injured woman's life. "Blood was everywhere with crying and moaning. I was on the phone with 911 reporting what had happened and while waiting we tried to stop the bleeding of those who we thought were still alive. Our chair got it the worst as he was right next to her along with the two others who died almost instantly. Six people sitting in the rows perpendicular to me were all shot fatally or seriously wounded."

Within minutes, a SWAT team arrived. A cacophony of sirens descended upon the quiet campus. City police. Campus police. Ambulances. It was pure mayhem.

Police radios crackled with a broadcast: "The female shooter is Doctor Amy Bishop. The shooter is Doctor Amy Bishop. Female. White. Dark hair. Blue Jeans."

Emergency workers raced into the conference room. It was a bloodbath. Moriarty was crying, shaking, describing how meticulously Bishop was shooting. Some of her colleagues wept. Others were stone faced. Shocked. Still trying to grapple with what they had just witnessed. Everyone noted Amy Bishop's look. How her face was fixed with rage.

"It was shoot, shoot, shoot, very regular, both hands on the gun," Moriarty reported. "She absolutely knew how to handle that gun."

Bishop knew enough to stash it, too. Police would learn that after the massacre she ran down a flight of stairs and into a second-floor ladies' bathroom. She stashed the gun in a trash can under the blood-soaked red plaid jacket that she had worn to class. She crumpled paper towels and threw the mess on top of the evidence.

Then she calmly walked into a classroom and asked to borrow someone's cell phone. Student Sean Tate handed the woman his. It struck the students as odd, but they had not heard the gun blasts above them.

"She looked anxious," Tate told *Dateline NBC*. "A lot of anxiety in her eyes really. But other than that, she looked like a normal person."

Bishop called her husband. "I'm done," she said. "Pick me up."

It was 4:05 p.m. Police radios continued to broadcast the BOLO—Be On The Lookout—for "Female Shooter. Doctor Amy Bishop." Campus cops raced around the campus and barked orders at students and faculty. There were at least 7,500 people on campus and they didn't want any one of them to confront the gunwoman who remained at large.

"Get in your cars! Lock the doors! Roll up the windows!"

The chaos was heightened when several members of the biology department flagged down a police commander.

"Sir, we have reason to believe that Amy Bishop may have booby-trapped the building with a herpes bomb," the cop was told.

"A what?"

"A herpes bomb," a professor said. "It was designed to spread the dangerous virus."

The concern had been raised by people who had worked alongside Bishop. She had done work with the herpes virus as a postdoctoral student. She had talked many times about how it could cause encephalitis. In fact, it was featured prominently in her novel *Amazon Fever*, which she had continued to work on vigorously in Alabama. It was a herpeslike virus that was spreading around the world in the novel causing pregnant women to miscarry. Bishop's coworkers were afraid for the police and urged them to be careful of anything strange that they saw.

By then the police had swept every room in the

building. There was no sign of a herpes bomb, but the idea that one may have been triggered in the building certainly further freaked out the already nervous police officers. A police officer radioed that he had found a gun and a red plaid jacket stained with blood stashed in a second-floor trash barrel. Police would soon find Bishop, too.

It was 4:09 p.m. A campus police officer spotted a strange woman wandering out of a maintenance entrance near a loading dock at the Shelby Center for Science and Technology. It was not a regular entrance, but a delivery area. The woman fit the description. Stocky. Heavyset. Her bangs were cut sharp across her forehead. Black hair. She was wearing faded blue jeans and a pink sweatshirt. She looked dazed. Maybe even deranged.

"Stop right there," the cop yelled. "You are under arrest."

Bishop stopped in her tracks. The cop snatched her arm and twisted it behind her back. He cuffed her hands. He picked up his police radio.

"Suspect is in custody. Repeat. Suspect is in custody. Female shooter Doctor Amy Bishop is in custody."

The cop put his hand on the top of her head, guiding her into the back of a Huntsville PD patrol car. A female cop stood at Bishop's side so she could not flee.

At 4:52 p.m., university officials e-mailed a message to UAH students and employees: "There has been a shooting on campus. The shooter has been apprehended. The campus is closed tonight. Everyone is encouraged to go home. Classes are canceled tonight. Any additional cancellations or changes will be announced as they become available." In short order, classes would be canceled for a week.

Grief counselors had been summoned. Students were alerted to their presence with e-mails that urged them to visit the counselors in rooms set aside for grieving. Many students would take advantage of the psychological aid. The dead had been popular. Dr. Gopi Podila had been a welcoming figure who was easy to relate to. Dr. Maria Ragland Davis, a professor of biotechnology and plant genomics, was recognized internationally for her work with third-world countries. Dr. Adriel Johnson was a professor of physiology who had an open-door policy and was known to stay well into the evening hours to answer his students' questions.

The names of the wounded were not immediately released. Students would learn that Dr. Joseph Leahy, professor of microbiology, was in critical condition. So was Stephanie Monticciolo, a staff assistant, described as the department den mother who nurtured both staff and students. Dr. Luis Cruz-Vera miraculously survived a gunshot wound to the chest. He was conscious and coherent. And angry.

James Anderson pulled up to the campus just before 5 p.m. to a sea of flashing lights. He watched emergency workers scramble to lift gurneys carrying full body bags into ambulances. A student passed him in a panic. Anderson asked him: "What happened? Did someone go crazy in the school?" The student ignored the question. Anderson stood by the side of his van and waited for Amy. He was worried for her.

"What are you doing here?" A Huntsville police officer had approached him. It was odd that the man was just standing there. But Bishop had rambled in the back of the police car as she was taken into custody: "I'm waiting for my husband. It's date night." The cop thought this might be that husband. Huntsville Police had been looking for him. He asked James Anderson again, "Sir. What are you doing here?"

"I'm waiting for my wife. What the hell is going on?"

"What is your name, sir?"

"James Anderson."

The cop broadcast that name over his police radio. By then, officers had spoken to students in the classroom that Bishop had burst into looking for a cell phone. Those students had heard her say, "Come pick me up." Police were waiting for him. "Sir, you're going to have to come with me."

With that, James Anderson was transported to the Huntsville Police Department's south precinct. He was put in a squad room for hours. He had no idea why he was there. "They just left me hanging," he said.

Cops had obtained a warrant within hours of the shooting. They seized Amy Bishop's computer at work. They searched the family's green clapboard home. As Anderson sat wondering why he was being detained, Lily, who was then eighteen, took her siblings to a neighbor's house.

At 10:15 p.m., an officer came into the room. "Your wife was involved in a shooting. Do you have any idea why your wife would shoot six people from her department?"

Anderson was stunned.

"Amy? Amy did that? She told me to pick her up. That it was date night."

The detective began to read a list of the names of the victims. Anderson stopped him. "I know these people," he said. "I don't want to know who died. I wish I did something. I didn't know she was going to do this."

Anderson was asked about the tenure problem. His wife's colleagues had told police that she was upset about it. That she constantly lamented the decision and had been very verbal about her dissatisfaction. Once again—just like the ATF agents who had investigated the letter bomb sent to the Harvard professor and the

Peabody police investigating the assault at the pancake house—investigators were puzzled. Amy Bishop had no history of violence. No police record. She seemed squeaky clean. The broom job of her brother's death had worked. No one in public safety would know that Amy Bishop had been busted with a gun before. A pump-action Mossberg that she had re-racked and fired three times in one afternoon back in December 1986.

When police began to question James Anderson at 10:15 p.m. that night, they had recovered Bishop's blood-soaked jacket and the 9-millimeter Ruger from the trash in the bathroom. It had been logged as evidence.

"Yeah, she was upset. But she had a Plan B. We were moving on. She was going to maybe go into full-time neuro-research. She was looking at other universities," Anderson told police.

"Do you own a gun, sir?" the detective asked.

Anderson paused before answering. "Yes. We were having problems with a neighbor and a buddy of mine bought me a gun in New Hampshire about twenty years ago. Massachusetts is full of kooks. There is a long waiting period. He did me a favor." Anderson didn't tell the cops that he had been shooting it with Amy. That they had gone to target practice for fun. That he had been worried about *her* being a victim of a school shooting.

By midnight, Anderson was home.

By then, his wife had been booked on capital murder charges. Police snapped a mug shot of her wearing a bulletproof vest that police had given her to wear in case anyone wanted to retaliate against her. It was standard operating procedure in Alabama. There were a lot of victims and it was not all that difficult to carry a firearm in the state. The cops did not want to take a chance that someone would exact their own justice. Throughout the booking process, Bishop denied being at the shooting scene. She expressed incredulousness that it had happened at all. "I wasn't there," she hold Huntsville homicide investigator Charles Gray. "It wasn't me." She said it over and over. They interviewed her for two hours. Of course, at one point during the questioning Bishop uttered the line she had repeated so often in her life.

"I am Doctor Amy Bishop. I didn't do anything. Why am I here? I have to get back to school and write a grant. I have a meeting at 4:30 p.m. I was not there. I didn't do anything. You can't hold me. I am Doctor Amy Bishop."

The officers ignored her, but noted her statements. After she was booked, police orchestrated a security motorcade so they could move her to the Madison County Jail. The extra security and the bulletproof vest were preventative. Cops did not want to take any chances that an angry family member would seek their own justice. Reporters crowded the outside of the police station before the move. As Bishop was led to an awaiting police car, they barked questions at her.

"Why did you do it? Why did you kill your colleagues?"

Bishop stared straight at them. "It didn't happen. There's no way."

Another question was fired at her. "What about the people who died?"

"There's no way. They're still alive," she said. With that, she was put into the cruiser and whisked away as part of a secure motorcade that would bring her to the jail.

There, she was strip-searched and then issued a red jumpsuit worn by high-security inmates and a pair of flip-flops. Her belongings were taken from her. Everything. Her shoes. Even her underwear. The jumpsuit would be worn against her bare skin. After she was processed as a new prisoner, she was moved into an eleven-by-fourteen-foot concrete cell at the Madison County Jail. Despite the carnage that she was accused of committing, Bishop dined on a turkey sandwich that she washed down with Kool-Aid that was delivered to her cell. She hadn't lost her appetite. There was not a single thing in her cell save for a Bible and a bare cot that she would sleep on. A prison guard would later bring her one blanket and one small pillow.

"Her situation allows for a lot of introspection," Madison County Chief Deputy Chris Stephens would tell reporters camped outside the jail that night. They wanted to see if anyone visited Bishop. She was placed on suicide watch, which was customary for inmates facing capital murder charges—likely in Bishop's case. The cold-blooded, calculated way in which Bishop's colleagues say she went about the killing spree fit the bill for a capital punishment charge. She had wiped out half the biology department in a matter of minutes. Three dead. Three critically wounded. Five others emotionally savaged, scarred for life.

"It's hard to get this image out of my mind," Ng told his friend that night. "I have mixed feelings of guilt and relief that I am alive or unharmed. Now half of our faculty is out of commission and we are wondering what to do."

Just after midnight, another e-mail went out. The university notified faculty and students that it would close the campus for a week. Early Saturday morning, James Anderson dropped by the school. He had been admonished not to leave town. The campus was a mess. Students had already set up a candlelit memorial and were huddled together even at that hour hugging and crying. He wanted to comfort them but knew it would be inappropriate. He drove home. The kids were still at the neighbor's.

James Anderson then sat alone on his couch and wept.

16

Braintree Police Chief Paul Frazier was sipping coffee and reading the online news on a Saturday morning when a report came in that piqued his interest. A Harvard-educated scientist had massacred several of her colleagues and had been taken into custody at the University of Alabama at Huntsville the day before. School shootings, sadly, had become so commonplace in the United States that the news registered alarm but no real surprise. It wasn't the three dead and three wounded that caught Chief Frazier's attention. It was the name of the scientist they had in custody. Frazier had been appointed chief of the Braintree Police well after his nemesis John Polio had retired.

"Female shooter is Doctor Amy Bishop."

As he read the story, his BlackBerry buzzed in his pocket. It was a text message from Deputy Chief Russell Jenkins. It read: "Karen thinks that's the same Amy Bishop who killed her brother." Karen was a lieutenant in the Braintree Police Department. Frazier called his deputy chief.

"We're looking for a picture of her right now from Huntsville PD," Jenkins told him. Minutes later, the chief's BlackBerry vibrated in his pocket. "It's her. Amy Bishop struck again."

Frazier was not surprised. He knew his friend retired Lieutenant Jay Sullivan would not be surprised
either. Sullivan was the only cop who wrote the word
"murder" on Bishop's paperwork. He was the one interviewing Bishop when her mother burst into the booking room twenty-four years earlier. The men had stayed
in touch after Sullivan's retirement and might even
share a coffee at the Braintree Dunkin' Donuts, which
was right around the corner from the former Bishop
house on Hollis Avenue. As a matter of fact, they talked
about that old case often. Frazier hated John Polio, the
former chief. The men hated each other. A lot of cops
hated Polio.

"Do you remember that crazy woman who had you
at gunpoint behind the Village News?" Frazier asked.
"The woman who killed her brother? Bishop?"

How could Sullivan forget? The case still rankled a
lot of the cops who had worked on it. In fact, even then it
was still a topic of conversation at the bar when the active and retired cops would meet up to trade war stories
about working for John Polio. It was an embarrass-
ment, the way that thing had been handled. Cops actually grumbled to one another, *Braintree, the city that
lets you get away with murder.*" That woman pointed
a loaded shotgun at police officers and got away with it.
She pointed the gun at workers at Dinger Ford and got
away with it. Hell, she shot her brother dead and got away
with it. Most cops blamed Polio and the then-district
attorney, Bill Delahunt. Now Delahunt was a United
States Congressman, a federal lawmaker. That was the
job that he had been after from the beginning. The cops
complained constantly that they were up against it with
those two in charge. Polio was a complete nutcase, they
claimed, and Delahunt, a self-serving bum.

Frazier asked Sullivan where he could locate the case file on the Bishop shooting. On his way into his office, Frazier called Braintree Mayor Joe Sullivan.

"Mayor, have you seen the news about the professor in Alabama [who] shot some of her colleagues?" Frazier asked him.

"No, I haven't," the Mayor responded.

"Well, we think it could be Amy Bishop. I'm not sure if you remember the incident where she shot her brother back in 1986."

The Mayor had never worked in law enforcement but remembered the case well. Everyone in Braintree did. It was an infamous story about Polio's strange stranglehold on the city that made him more like a small-town sheriff than a politically driven police chief.

Mayor Joe Sullivan was fairly new to the job and wanted to make sure he was briefed extensively. He listened as Frazier recalled the details of Bishop's brief arrest. How Polio had called the then-Captain Theodore Buker and ordered Amy Bishop released. How the cops were livid. For cripes sake, the girl had her coat on in the house and "accidentally" fired a very powerful shotgun three separate times. There was an article on her bedroom floor about a very similar crime from the *National Enquirer.* The mayor was sold. He called current District Attorney Bill Keating, and set up a meeting. He wanted answers.

At the Braintree police station, the cops were abuzz about the Bishop arrest. They had seen her mug shot on the news. Braintree Police Lieutenant Karen MacAleese had the picture in her hand. She had gone to high school with Amy Bishop. Bishop looked about the same. "Oh, that's the same Amy Bishop," MacAleese told her chief. "No doubt about it." Frazier was furious. Almost as mad as he had been the night he'd been told by cops that Amy Bishop's mother stormed into an interview room and demanded that her daughter be released.

Frazier made his way to a locked trailer that stored the department's day logs stretching back decades. He found the entries for December 6, 1986. Most of the entries were run-of-the-mill calls. A B&E (breaking and entering) case. A sudden death. An alarm sounded at a closed pharmacy. A motor vehicle accident. Another B&E. It was all entered in cursive. Frazier found what he was looking for. Case number 864718.

"14:22, 46 Hollis Ave, accidental shooting. Sudden death. Sgt. Brady responding.

"15:07, Victim of shooting died at QCH [Quincy City Hospital]."

Not a word about Bishop's arrest. Nothing about the gunpoint standoff with police or the attempted carjackings.

Frazier photocopied the information. Then he locked the original book in his office. Couldn't be too careful. He walked over to a section of the building that had once served as the firing range. Now the department stored archived files there. Frazier looked at the pile of boxes and sucked in a breath. Just then Ron Solimini walked in. He had been the officer menaced by Bishop as she held firm to the loaded shotgun. His grandfather had been the retiring cop who wanted to stay on the job until he was seventy, the captain that Amy Bishop's mother had defended months before the shooting.

"Hey—you see that case with Bishop and your father?" Frazier asked him.

"Good luck," Solimini said. "That thing disappeared way back in [the] eighties. You're not going to find it. The old chief tried. That thing got buried real good."

The cops started to look through the files together.

They found a box labeled December 1986 and pulled it out. There had been a case number assigned to the shooting from the log Frazier photocopied. But as he flipped through the box, it became clear that Solimini was right. The file was gone.

"Jesus," Frazier told Solimini. "You're right. The reports are gone. This is unbelievable."

Frazier called the Huntsville Police Department. The investigators in Alabama should know who they were really dealing with. Because Bishop never logged a police record—the pancake house punch arrest was squashed after she stayed out of trouble for six months—the investigators working on the rampage at the school would have no idea that Bishop had a violent history. He picked up his cell phone and dialed the Huntsville Police Chief. He left a voicemail and then reached out to the dispatcher.

"Hi. My name is Paul Frazier and I am the police chief in Braintree, Massachusetts. I'm calling in regard to yesterday's shooting," he told the dispatcher.

"Yes, sir. We're busy," the dispatcher said, impatiently. "How can I help you?"

"Well, I believe the Amy Bishop you have in custody is the same Amy Bishop who grew up in Braintree. I think you should know she shot and killed her brother back in 1986."

There was a long pause from the dispatcher. She told him to hang on. Frazier heard a muffled conversation between the dispatcher and a Huntsville officer. "I have some crazy guy on the phone who said the woman who killed all the professors killed her brother in his town a few years ago."

Frazier waited. The dispatcher got back on the line. "Sir, where are you calling from?"

"I know this sounds crazy," Frazier explained. "But

I believe the woman you have in custody, Amy Bishop, is the same person who shot and killed her brother in Braintree, Massachusetts, in 1986."

The dispatcher transferred Frazier to the Huntsville Homicide Division. There he got a sergeant. "I just want to make sure she doesn't get bailed without you knowing what she did here," Frazier told him.

"Bailed?" the sergeant was incredulous. Then again, he worked in Alabama, not notoriously liberal Massachusetts.

"Well, in Massachusetts she'd probably be home by now."

The sergeant almost laughed. "Are you people nuts up there?"

"What can I tell you? It's Massachusetts."

The Huntsville homicide sergeant and the Braintree Police Chief exchanged information.

Braintree police alerted the media that Frazier would be having a press conference that would pertain to the recent arrest of Harvard University–educated Amy Bishop, who was a native of Braintree. Reporters, of course, had been frantically chasing down the story of the mad scientist, the nutty professor. The woman's mug shot helped sell the story on the nightly news and on the front pages of newspapers. She looked crazy, with her freaky eyes and hand-groomed bangs. The Harvard connection was just icing on the cake. They had found the one short story in the archives of the *Patriot Ledger* about Seth Bishop's accidental shooting. It was shocking, but it would pale in comparison with what Chief Frazier was about to drop.

The conference room at the Braintree Police station was packed with reporters, even on a Saturday. For Frazier, this was an opportunity to vindicate the men who had worked for him and alongside him on that December day, the men who had risked their lives apprehending the young Amy Bishop and the men who had been thwarted in their efforts to bring her to justice. Frazier wore his freshly pressed white uniform shirt. His blue tie sported a standard-issue gold Marine Corps clasp. It was a reminder to his cops that in the Marines Frazier learned that he would protect his rank and file over his own job—even if that meant he was going to piss off a few politicians. He stepped to a podium decorated with the Braintree PD emblem and began to speak:

"Good afternoon. The members of the Braintree Police Department extend their thoughts and prayers to the victims in the shooting incident which occurred at the University of Alabama, in Huntsville, Alabama, as well as to their families and the members of the Huntsville Police Department who responded to and are investigating the incident.

"I have been in contact with the Huntsville Police Department to confirm that the suspect in their shooting had been involved in a shooting incident in Braintree twenty-four years ago. Their investigators will be back in touch with us within a couple of days.

"The suspect in the Huntsville shooting, Amy Bishop, had been involved in a shooting incident in Braintree, Massachusetts, in December of 1986. I located the day log from December of 1986 and found that the incident had occurred on December 6th. After finding the report number I looked in our archived files for the report. I was unable to locate the report.

"Officer Ronald Solimini informed me that he wrote the report and said that I wouldn't find it, as it has been missing from the files for over twenty years. He said that former Police Chief Edward Flynn had looked for the report and that it was missing. He believes this was in 1988.

"Officer Solimini recalled the incident as follows: He said he remembers that Ms. Bishop fired a round from a pump-action shotgun into the wall of her bedroom. She had a fight with her brother and shot him, which caused his death. She fired a third round from the shotgun into the ceiling as she exited the home. She fled down the street with the shotgun in her hand. At one point she allegedly pointed the shotgun at a motor vehicle in an attempt to get the driver to stop. Officer Solimini found her behind a business on Washington Street. Officer Timothy Murphy was able to take control of the suspect at gunpoint and seized the shotgun. Ms. Bishop was subsequently handcuffed and transported to the police station under arrest.

"Officer Solimini informed me that before the booking process was completed, Ms. Bishop was released from custody without being charged.

"I spoke with the retired deputy chief who was then a lieutenant and was responsible for booking Ms. Bishop. He said he had started the process when he received a phone call he believes was from then-Police Chief John Polio, or possibly from a captain on Chief Polio's behalf. He was instructed to stop the booking process. At some point, Ms. Bishop was turned over to her mother and they left the building via a rear exit.

"Braintree Police Lieutenant Karen MacAleese was a high school classmate and confirmed from photographs that the suspect is the same Amy Bishop who lived in Braintree.

"I was not on duty at the time of the incident, but I recall how frustrated the members of the department were over the release of Ms. Bishop. It was a difficult time for the department as there had been three shooting incidents within a short timeframe. The release of Ms. Bishop did not sit well with the police officers, and I can assure you that this would not happen in this day and age.

"It is troubling that this incident has come to light. I can assure you that the members of the Braintree Police Department maintain the highest level of integrity. Since it was discovered this morning that the report is missing, I have been in contact with Mayor Joseph Sullivan. Mayor Sullivan and I have spoken with District Attorney William Keating and we will be meeting with him next week to discuss this situation. The mayor supports a full review of this matter and agrees that we want to know where the records are."

Frazier took a few questions from the startled press.

"Chief, what happened?" yelled *Boston Herald* crime reporter O'Ryan Johnson. "Was this a cover-up?"

"I don't want to use the word 'cover-up,'" Frazier said. "I don't know what the thought process was of the police chief at the time."

With that, Frazier ended the news conference.

Reporters wanted to know what the thought process of the old police chief was, too. So they drove right to his house.

17

In his time, Chief John Polio was the most powerful man in Braintree, usurping even the mayor. Everyone was afraid of him. He was unpredictable; he would take a certain relish in finding creative ways to take down his enemies, some cops said. He had fired cops because they had tattoos. He had raided old ladies' Beano games because they were unlicensed. He locked up the town tax collector and a state representative for drunk driving—unheard of in Massachusetts, where politicians enjoyed a time-honored immunity for a lot of crimes, especially DUI. He shut down firefighter-run casino nights that raised money for charities and told the Braintree Women's Club they could not sell lottery tickets to subsidize scholarships they offered. He painted the Braintree patrol cars different colors so he could keep track of his officers, earning the city's police the unflattering moniker "Rainbow Fleeters." There would be vulgar graffiti scrawled about Polio in town. He had never been considered a nice guy. He was so loathed that in 1984 someone threw a firebomb into his unmarked police car parked in his driveway at 1:15 in the morning. He was asleep in his house. So were two of his daughters and two tenants. His wife had left him. In the days after the cruiser burst into flames, ominous calls were placed to the police station, according to a profile of the chief that ran in the *Patriot Ledger* that year. "Polio is with the wrong woman," the caller hissed. "Polio and his girlfriend will be blown up." Polio denied having a girlfriend and wrote the arson off as an attempt to publicly humiliate him. The crime was never solved. And Polio didn't spend much time worrying about it. He had made a lot of enemies in his lifetime. One of them was Bill Delahunt. Ordinarily, political squabbles were kept fairly quiet. Polio was not that kind of man, though. In the 1984 *Ledger* profile, he attacked Delahunt as a political sacred cow. "He's a hanger-on . . . if he has a political future, it's a sad commentary on our society." Those remarks were made eleven years before Delahunt became a U.S. representative.

That was then. On February 13, 2010, he just looked like a broken-down old man. He was eighty-seven years old, and he looked it. Scrawny and weather-beaten. When the doorbell rang, he came to the door wearing a baseball hat that read *No. 1 Grandpa*. He knew they would be coming. He had received a courtesy call from Mayor Joe Sullivan after Frazier's press conference.

"The press is probably on their way, John," the mayor told him. Then he asked if he could see Polio. The retired chief told him, "I'm retired. I'm not going to be ordered to Town Hall by anyone."

The mayor was right about the press. Polio saw the news trucks pull up. He went to the door and invited the reporters in. He then settled onto his sofa and pulled a fleece blanket over his lap.

"What do you all want?"

With that came a flurry of questions. Reporters were drowning one another out with rapid-fire inquiries. Polio admonished them, "One at a time."

"Was there a cover-up in the Seth Bishop shooting?"

Polio guffawed. "What's a cover-up?" He continued: "The way I remember it, that girl and her brother were horseplaying around with the family shotgun. It went off. That boy was blasted in the chest. The idea that it's clandestine, it's missing, a cover-up . . . is so outlandish, it's ridiculous," he said. He was furious about Frazier's press conference and he let reporters know it.

"There was inferences, not so subtle, that there was a cover-up," Polio said. "That irked me a little bit, because nothing could be further from the truth. And I had also hoped that the chief would extend that courtesy to me and give me a call—give me a heads-up that the press was coming here, en masse, and get an explanation from me of the questions he had."

What about her fleeing from the home? What about the attempted holdup of the men at Dinger Ford? What about the gunpoint standoff Amy had with his Braintree cops? What about the fact that the weapon was loaded? That she had a shell in her pocket? That she had her winter coat on? Why was her mother allowed to sneak her out a back door? Why wasn't she arrested? Why wasn't she charged? Where are the missing reports?

Polio brushed off all the questions. He just didn't remember a thing, he said. His memory was blank. Nothing rang a bell.

In his phone call, the mayor asked Polio if he could locate the missing records. Polio was unhelpful, according to cops. By late Saturday afternoon, the State Police report filed by Brian Howe, the investigator from the Norfolk District Attorney's office at the time, was located in the archives. That was all they had, however. DA Bill Keating's press secretary, David Traub, reminded reporters that the mess had been created long before his boss had been voted into office. "Since there are no police investigators or prosecutors presently in our office who were involved in the investigation in 1986–87, that archival material constitutes the information at our disposal," Traub said.

The suggestion, of course, was that reporters who wanted answers would have to reach out to the former Norfolk County DA, William Delahunt, now a U.S. representative for the South Shore's 10th Congressional District. But Delahunt wasn't talking. His office put out a statement that the congressman was on a six-day trip in the Middle East and could not be reached for comment. Of course not. Apparently there were no phones in the Middle East? Delahunt had never been one for accountability, many of the veteran reporters knew, and they expected he'd be ducking questions on this matter, as he had so many times in the past.

Howe's report was handed over to Frazier and Mayor Sullivan. Polio was given a copy, too. He used it to bolster his argument that he had acted appropriately when he ordered Amy Bishop to be released. He blamed his former captain, Theodore Buker, for the mess. Buker was a convenient scapegoat. He had died thirteen years earlier. "It was ruled accidental, as I said, and we had forwarded whatever records we had. Everything was done correctly by the Braintree police," Polio announced.

The old police chief would eat those words. Within days the current DA, Bill Keating, would make an announcement of his own.

18

On the Sunday morning after the rampage, James Anderson woke up his children. Their house had been ringed with reporters since Friday evening. There were camera crews and still photographers and news anchors and crime scribes. The scene was absolutely insane. James planned to stay in the house—as he had since he cried on the couch in the early morning hours the day before—and hope that his life was as normal as it had been on Thursday. That day, Amy had gone to work. The kids had gone to school. He had worked with business partners at Prodigy on the petri dish unveiling, which was slated to happen in a matter of months.

It was hard to believe that his family's life as they knew it was destroyed. Completely destroyed. Of course, the Bishops had been calling the house all weekend. Judy must have called fifty times on Saturday. James guessed it was understandable. The charges against their daughter had not yet been announced. The media did report that a gun had been recovered in the second-floor bathroom and that Amy was on suicide watch in the county jail.

"Judy," James told her when he finally answered the phone. "I just don't know anything. I haven't seen her. I haven't talked to her. I have to go."

His parents were on their way. They had heard about the shooting on the news. It was on in the background. They weren't paying that much attention to it. "Another goddamn school shooting," Jim Anderson Sr. mumbled to himself. Then his wife Sandy spotted the woman who was put into a police cruiser.

"That's Amy!" she exclaimed.

"Jesus Christ," her husband said. "Jesus H. Christ."

Anderson hung up on Judy Bishop and the phone rang again. He sighed. He changed his mind. Tired of the phone ringing, tired of the reporters outside, he decided he wanted to take the kids to church. That's what they did every Sunday. Go to church and then watch Netflix videos as a family. The Andersons belonged to two Christian nondenominational churches. Amy had found religion in Alabama. It was how people in those parts socialized, she knew, and she wanted her children to have friends. She did not want them living the solitary life of geeky child. She wanted her kids to be smart and popular. Church was a good way to make sure they were part of the community. Besides, at UAH that type of "community involvement" was known to help in the tenure process. There were a lot of church folk at her university.

James Anderson wanted the day to be as ordinary as it could be for the kids, especially Seth, who was only eight now. The phone kept ringing. Judy Bishop was just as stubborn as her daughter. At that moment, she and her husband were holed up in Ipswich. They still lived in the Birch Lane house where their daughter had been such a cantankerous neighbor. Sam's prostate cancer was persistent and the news had made him even more uncomfortable. Amy Bishop might have been a pain in the ass, but her parents had never given anyone any problems. Neighbors felt sorry for them. They had no idea the Bishops had lost a son until the recent news reports. It certainly explained a lot about their daughter, who was now on suicide watch.

They would bring the Bishops groceries and shield them from the reporters who had staked out the house now for days. James Anderson knew all this because of the umpteen phone calls he had gotten from his mother-in-law. The phone rang nonstop, and it was ringing again. *Damn it*, he said to himself. Then he picked up.

"Judy. I have to go," James said without waiting to hear the voice on the other end of the phone.

"James?"

It was Amy calling from the county jail. James sucked in a breath. He didn't know what to say.

"I know you guys are obviously in shock. I can't say much. They monitor these phones," she said.

"Are you okay?" he asked.

"I'm okay. Are the kids okay? Did they do their homework? Are they eating? Does Seth miss me?"

James Anderson again had to take a deep breath. *Did the kids do their homework?* What kind of question was that? The cops had ransacked their rooms. Reporters were hounding them with questions. The TV was blaring updates on the mad professor who went on a shooting rampage. The last thing their children were thinking of was homework.

"I love you, James."

Anderson hung up the phone without saying another word. They had been married twenty years. He had fallen in love with her in an instant at a Dungeons & Dragons event. They held hands there for the first time and she asked him, "Do you want to do nothing together?" He loved that line. Sure, their relationship had its issues. She was strong-willed and opinionated and hard to get along with. Maybe even a little domineering. But they had shared the same interests from the time they were young adults dating. Science fiction conferences and movies. *Star Trek* conventions. They spoke the same language scientifically. He loved her. He had always felt like he knew his wife, truly knew her.

Not today. News of the startling press conference back in Braintree, Massachusetts, had made its way to television broadcasts in Alabama. As the truth filtered out about how Amy Bishop's little brother had died back in 1986, Anderson began to wonder if he had ever really known his wife at all.

19

All across Huntsville, flags flew at half-mast to honor the dead and wounded UAH employees: across the campus of the University of Alabama, and on public buildings throughout the city, by order of Huntsville Mayor Tommy Battle. "We share our thoughts and prayers with the families of the victims. May God bless them and comfort them in this time of grief," Battle said in a statement. The shrine of candles and flowers outside the Shelby Building—where the massacre had broken out in a third-floor conference room—had grown into a monument to the slain. Three female students had already covered a sidewalk under a flagpole in front of the Shelby Building in chalk writing: GOD BLESS UAH and PROUD TO BE A CHARGER!

As Anderson prepared to take his children to church, mourners got ready for a prayer vigil on campus. Word had leaked that Amy Bishop had been officially charged by police. She was being held on three counts of capital murder and three charges of attempted murder. She would face the death penalty.

Hundreds of faculty, students, and friends crowded into the UAH University Center. They were grief-stricken. Some of them were angry. Not only had Amy Bishop been responsible for the death of her brother in a case that was now raising eyebrows, it was now being reported that she had been a suspect in an assassination attempt on her former professor at Harvard in 1993. And now another story had emerged that Bishop had attacked a woman at an IHOP a year before she was hired as an associate UAH professor. How did the school miss these warning signs?

Those questions would be put aside, at least for a couple of hours. The prayer service was not about trying to place blame on anyone—even though it certainly seemed that investigators in Massachusetts had raised questions that needed to be answered. It was about comfort.

"You always ask 'Why?' in a situation like this," Huntsville police spokesman Sergeant Mark Roberts said before the vigil began. "There may never be an answer to that."

Those assembled sang "Let There Be Peace on Earth." Then there were clergy from five different religions who recited prayers for peace. All denominations were represented, which was appropriate given the diversity that existed among the victims. University President Dave Williams began the service by saying that grief had led to loss of sleep and loss of appetite across campus, but that shock was an appropriate counterbalance to selfish and destructive motives. Williams had spent the day before at the hospital and at the homes of the victims expressing his condolences. "We will face this tragedy together, we will learn from this experience, and we will emerge with strength and confidence," Williams told the congregation.

No one who spoke mentioned Bishop by name.

Dr. Laj Utreja led the group in a Hindu prayer. He had been friendly with Dr. Podila. Both scientists had attended the same temple. "He was a world-class scientist," the UAH professor told the assembled crowd. "For this community, this is a great loss."

Dr. Moriarty felt blessed. She had survived the death of her husband, Joe Howard, who died of throat cancer when their daughter was only eleven years old. She had survived breast cancer five years before that gun would be pointed at her and fired—with no bullets. She had survived the carnage that unfolded in front of her. She was a fighter. She believed that God and the Holy Spirit had saved her and she wanted to share her blessings. She would do so by talking to the press. She was already being heralded as a hero by survivors. She had grabbed Bishop's leg and led her to the doorway. Who knows how many others Bishop would have shot if Moriarty had not done that? She was the UAH Dean of Graduate Studies and had always been a warm, welcoming presence on campus. Besides, it was cathartic to talk about what she went through. Now that she had had a few days to process the attack, she remembered that Bishop had been uncharacteristically quiet during Friday's faculty meeting. It was also odd that she had come at all, considering that she would not be part of the faculty come spring, and the meeting was focused on the following year's budget. A *Huntsville Times* reporter asked Moriarty after the prayer vigil why she had grabbed Amy Bishop's leg. Wasn't she scared?

"What are you going to do? A person's standing there shooting. You've got to do something." Moriarty vowed that she was going to go back to teaching. She had already visited Dr. Luis Cruz-Vera, who had been grazed by a bullet. He was treated and released from the hospital the day after the shooting. Joseph Leahy remained in critical condition in the neuro ICU at Huntsville Hospital. Department secretary Stephanie Monticciolo was in serious condition in the hospital's surgical intensive care unit.

Dr. Ng had grown up in Los Angeles and was accustomed to violence in the headlines. He had never expected it in the city he had called home for eleven years. "It's quite devastating," he told reporters. "One day you have all these great people working with you," he said. "Next day: They're gone."

20

Back in Massachusetts on Monday morning, Braintree Mayor Joe Sullivan told reporters that the city's police officers had spent the weekend after the UAH shootings looking for the missing police records on the Amy Bishop case. "We are digging," Sullivan said. "It's a long discovery process. We've been working all through the weekend." Sullivan then released a statement for the frustrated Braintree residents who were asking how the case could have been so mishandled.

"The Town of Braintree wishes to express its sincere and heartfelt condolences to the families of the victims of the shootings at the University of Alabama at Huntsville. In response to the arrest of Amy Bishop, the town of Braintree and its police department, in conjunction with the Norfolk County District Attorney's Office, is conducting a full and thorough review of its municipal and law enforcement records to locate all materials relating to the December 6, 1986 death of Seth Bishop.

"The town of Braintree and its police department recognizes the importance of transparency in the conduct of its affairs. The Braintree police department will conduct a thorough audit of all its records to identify if there were deficits in its past record-keeping process. It is important to note that in 1986, police records were created and maintained manually, which complicates their review and retrieval. The technology currently employed by the Braintree police department ensures that records are properly preserved.

"The results of this review, when completed, will be shared with relevant law enforcement agencies and the public."

The mayor's statement would be of little comfort to the Braintree cops, both active and retired, who believed the case file had been deliberately removed from their archives.

William Delahunt was still in hiding. He refused to answer any questions. Staffers continued to push the line that he was unavailable due to his overseas trip. The excuse was absurd in an era of worldwide cell phone coverage and e-mail, but Delahunt's aides were sticking to it. An *Associated Press* reporter tracked Delahunt down at a public event in Tel Aviv on Wednesday, February 17, 2010—five days after the UAH shooting. Delahunt brushed off questions, saying he did not have a clear recollection of the case. He told reporters to talk to his top prosecutor, John Kivlan, saying the Bishop case had been his responsibility.

"I understand I haven't had a real opportunity to get into the details of the case, but I suspect when I return I'll have an opportunity to become debriefed, and I know there have been statements, but I'm not really in a position to see any records," Delahunt said in Tel Aviv. He was there with a Congressional delegation sponsored by J Street, a Jewish lobbying group that was advocating for a Palestinian state.

John Kivlan, the former first prosecutor for Bill Delahunt, passed the blame onto Braintree police, saying in a statement: "Why the Braintree Police Department did not seek complaints in the Quincy District Court on the above charges is unknown to me."

Delahunt's spokesman also weighed in: "There was information that was not made available to the state police and the District Attorney's Office that was very significant. These are very serious questions that need to be addressed."

By then the current DA, Bill Keating, had conducted his own investigation of the records. His prosecutors determined that there was at least enough evidence to charge Amy Bishop with three crimes on December 6, 1986. They included assault with a deadly weapon for holding the gun on an employee of a nearby auto body shop in an attempt to secure a getaway car, possession of a firearm, and possession of ammunition. The statute of limitations on those crimes had expired. However, there was no statute of limitations on murder.

The news rekindled old rumors about Judy Bishop's role in the investigation. Braintree town clerk Joseph Powers revealed that Bishop served as a town meeting member from 1980 to 1993. She and her husband, Sam, served for a year on the town's arts lottery council for a year in 1985. Those appointments gave the couple significant political sway. At that time, the way the town's government worked was that the 240 town meeting members approved the municipal budget, as well as bylaw and zoning changes. As a town meeting member, Judy Bishop had power over Police Chief John Polio's budget. She had been a player in the town for six years when her son was shot. In fact, it was well-known that at a town meeting months before the shooting, Judy Bishop had loudly backed a Braintree police captain named Charles Solimini who wanted to stay on the job for five years beyond the mandatory retirement age. No one knew then that just months later, Judy Bishop's daughter would end up training a loaded shotgun on Solimini's son Ron, and that it would be Ron who handcuffed her after the standoff.

While Delahunt remained in the Middle East, Braintree Police Chief Paul Frazier found the police reports at the home of the late Ted Buker, the captain who had been ordered by Polio to release Amy Bishop. Buker had died on September 14, 1993. No one knew why he had the files secreted at his house in a box labeled CAPTAIN BUKER MAJOR CASE FILES. His family had heard the news of the missing files after Frazier's press conference and had given the box to the police chief. Sure enough, the original Bishop reports were in there. The pages were stained with rust from the aging paper clips. But they were intact. The documents—just as cops remembered—all had "accidental shooting" written across the top. That's what they said they had been ordered to write by Buker more than two decades before. The booking form where Lt. Jay Sullivan had classified the case as a murder was never found.

Frazier called the mayor's chief of staff, Peter Morin.

"Found the reports," Frazier said.

"Where?" Morin asked. Frazier told him. Morin sighed.

"I can't deal with the mayor tonight," Frazier said. "I'll have the reports delivered to Town Hall." He sent a patrolman to the mayor's office with copies of the paperwork. Within minutes of the delivery, he got a call that summoned him to Braintree Town Hall the next morning. There he found the town solicitor, Carolyn Murray; the mayor; Morin; Frazier; and his deputy chief, Russell Jenkins. The mayor was still a little peeved at Frazier for not giving him a heads-up about the press conference. He was mad that Polio had not been invited to defend himself in the case. Everyone in town knew there was bad blood between the two men and Sullivan did not want to appear to take a side in the battle. When Frazier arrived at Town Hall, the Mayor grilled him for hours about the incident. Frazier had been on the job for seventeen years, but the mayor was still getting his feet wet. He appeared annoyed that Frazier had upstaged him in the media this early in his tenure. "No more press," he told his police chief. After that, Joe Sullivan called Bill Keating. The men knew one another a bit from South Shore political circles, but they hadn't had much interaction since Sullivan took the mayor's job. Sullivan hung up the phone and looked a little rattled.

"We are going to Keating's office," he said. Those assembled made the drive to the Norfolk County District Attorney's Office in Canton. They were shown into a conference room. The mayor demanded that the cops turn off their cell phones. He didn't want to be embarrassed. The veteran police commanders exchanged eye rolls. *Who did this guy think he was talking to?*

Keating had one message for all of them: Stop talking. That included Sullivan. Keating was going to ask for an inquest into the case. Maybe Amy Bishop was finally going to face a murder charge after all. Braintree cops, both active and retired, were all too happy to help. Especially if it meant exposing Delahunt. Police officers had long complained about his reign as DA. They hated that the art thief Myles Connor had beaten the murder rap. And they loathed the way the Bishop investigation had been dropped, which they claimed would have been possible only with the help of a complicit district attorney. It was Delahunt's responsibility to speak for the dead. Seth Bishop never had a voice. The cops were stunned when Delahunt was quoted as saying from the Middle East: "I know the buck stops with me, but I never got the buck." How lame was that?

When Sullivan called Polio and told him the records had been found at the dead captain's house, Polio was shocked. The records started a new round of accusations between Polio and Delahunt's people. Polio continued to blame the deceased Buker as well, claiming the captain had made the ultimate decision. "Captain Buker recounted it to me, and we sent it to the district attorney's office," Polio said. "Why blame us? The district attorney has ultimate jurisdiction in this case, why not give it to him?"

The old man then began to stammer. "I was convinced it was an accident," he said to Sullivan, a statement he would repeat to reporters. Every time Polio was interviewed he wore his *No. 1 Grandpa* baseball cap. "Captain Buker told me it was an accident. That was the information that I had."

"Now," he added, "I'm not so sure."

21

In Alabama, the outrage had hit a boiling point. With each passing day came more information about how Massachusetts officials had let Amy Bishop off the hook in connection with a string of serious crimes. "We're very angry," said Jennifer Davis, whose brother-in-law's wife was the first victim of Amy Bishop's rampage. Davis was eager to express her family's fury and had reached out to a *Huntsville Times* reporter. "She took lives. If they [Massachusetts officials] knew she had problems maybe they could have done something. Look how many lives were taken."

Even the Huntsville Police expressed surprise at just how botched the investigation into Seth Bishop's death had been. Ordinarily, police agencies protect one another. But after reading the Braintree Police reports any cop could see that Amy Bishop should have faced at least a grand jury investigation back in 1986. "If Massachusetts authorities had done what they were supposed to do in the beginning, this might not have happened," said Huntsville sergeant Mark Roberts.

It was an old story: a community furious that a violent Massachusetts con who belonged in prison had instead wreaked havoc on their lives. The state did not earn the nickname "Laxachusetts" from a New Hampshire newspaper editorial for nothing. That writer was responding to the case of a Manchester, New Hampshire police officer named Michael Briggs who had been gunned down by a career criminal and Boston gang member, Michael "Stix" Addison, in 2006. The state's Attorney General Kelly Ayotte described Addison as "engaging in a continuing pattern of criminal and violent conduct, has threatened others with violence and has demonstrated low rehabilitative potential." His rap sheet proved that. Addison was only twenty-seven but had committed a plethora of violent crimes and served very little time in jail. His record included convictions on two violent armed attacks in Boston's Dorchester and Roxbury neighborhoods in the 1990s; he was also accused in a shooting and a pair of holdups in Manchester and Nashua in the six days preceding Michael L. Briggs's murder. New Hampshire residents were furious at the lax attitude that the courts had shown Addison in Massachusetts. A similar scenario played out in Washington state a year after the cop killing. A savage killer named Daniel Tavares—who had been locked up in Massachusetts for hacking his own mother to death with a kitchen knife—was released over the objections of prosecutors and prison shrinks. Before he murdered his own mom, he had racked up arrests for other acts of brutality. Upon his release in 2007, Tavares married his prison pen pal and relocated to Washington. Within a matter of weeks, he had an argument with his new neighbors, a young newlywed couple, over a $50 tattoo drawing. He shot them dead.

"It's because of stupidity in Massachusetts that my daughter is dead," said Darrel Slater, fifty-five, as he prepared to bury his daughter, Beverly Mauck, twenty-eight, and her husband, Brian Mauck, thirty. "How did they let him out?"

That question had been asked of Massachusetts authorities over and over again. In fact, a similar story garnered national outrage that would end the presidential aspirations of Democratic Governor Michael Dukakis. On June 6, 1986, a notorious killer named Willie Horton, who was in jail for life without parole, was released from his jail cell as part of a weekend furlough program. He never came back. On April 3, 1987 in Oxon Hill, Maryland, Horton twice raped a local woman after pistol-whipping, knifing, binding, and gagging her fiancé. He then stole the car belonging to the man he had assaulted. He was later captured by police after a chase. On October 20, Horton was sentenced in Maryland to two consecutive life terms plus eighty-five years. The sentencing judge, Vincent J. Femia, refused to return Horton to Massachusetts, saying, "I'm not prepared to take the chance that Mr. Horton might again be furloughed or otherwise released. This man should never draw a breath of free air again."

It was certainly understandable that the Maryland judge felt that way. Massachusetts was notorious. In 2009, cop killer Terrell Muhammad walked out of a Massachusetts prison. The forty-seven-year-old had killed a woman working in a record store twenty years earlier. He was released after serving a paltry five years in prison for the killing of that young mom. In 1994, he would kill again; this time his target was Boston police officer named Thomas Rose, shot dead in a BPD station house. Cops around the country were appalled when Muhammad was freed on National Police Officers Memorial Day—May 15, 2009—after serving about half his sentence for manslaughter. Not surprisingly, Muhammad was arrested less than a year later in Rhode Island when he tried to run over two Cranston, Rhode Island, police officers who were attempting to arrest him.

Before that he had been busted for stealing flat-screen TVs from a veterans' hospital. Rose's son who carried on his father's legacy by joining the BPD, was appalled. But not shocked. "It literally makes you sick to see how criminals are treated in Massachusetts," said Boston patrolman Tom Rose Jr. "I see it all the time and it's nauseating. When are we going to wake up?"

In Alabama, family members of the dead and the wounded were stunned that UAH had not done its job in vetting Bishop. "Were they so impressed that she graduated from Harvard that they put us all in danger?" Ng, who continued to suffer from the trauma of what he witnessed in that conference room, would ask. "It's a legitimate question and should be investigated."

On February 19, 2010, UAH biology department chair Gopi Podila was remembered during a Hindu funeral ceremony. It was packed. More than a thousand people gathered to mourn him. "His loss is felt all over the world," Alabama A&M University biology professor Ramesh Kantety told the congregation. But even as Podila was remembered, authorities in Massachusetts were criticized. "People kept sweeping her [Amy Bishop] bad behavior under the rug and we are paying a tremendous price for that," one Podila relative said through tears.

A quiet memorial service was held on February 20, 2010 in the Chan Auditorium at UAH. The service was held by the Minority Graduate Student Association to honor the two African-American professors who were gunned down: Dr. Maria Ragland Davis and Dr. Adriel Johnson Sr. The two were founders of the Council of African-American Faculty on campus and had helped countless students "dream their dreams and live them," one student remembered. Davis was a jazz lover and wrote poems when she was not teaching biology. Johnson was the master of "giving constructive criticism," a student shared. The congregation laughed in appreciation.

Later that night, thousands of people would crowd a massive service on campus. It was held at Spragins Hall Auditorium. There would be extensive coverage in the *Huntsville Times*. The dead were named one by one. Each name brought the sound of a single chime. The UAH Concert Choir broke out in the sorrowful song, "Alleluia." Professor Letha Etzkorn, president of the faculty senate, tried to offer a peaceful message. "I think it's impossible to have hatred in your heart when you're watching the snow fall. I wish the snow had been falling on campus last Friday."

Professor Sonja Brown-Givens asked, "How do we go back to normal?" and then answered her own question. "I don't think it's possible. Not for a while."

Unlike the previous memorial, at this prayer meeting Bishop would be mentioned twice. "We cannot understand Amy's actions," said campus chaplain Rev. Natalie Bennett. "But we pray for her and her family. Her innocent children."

The campus reopened the day after the memorial. It was a strange Monday morning. The mood was melancholy. Some, however, were shocked to see Lily Bishop Anderson, the shooter's eighteen-year-old daughter, back on campus. She was a genetics student attending classes for free because her mother was a professor there. It was one thing to see her on campus. It was another thing to see her in the lab of Dr. Adriel Johnson—a professor whom her mother was accused of murdering. Her classmates tittered. She didn't mind a bit. Her grandfather, Jim Anderson Sr.—who was taking care of the kids along with his wife and son—defended her. "Why would that be a problem?" he asked. "She didn't do it. Her mother did. She is a real sweetie-pie and should not be punished for what her mother did."

Attending classes was one thing. UAH administrators could not boot Lily Bishop Anderson off campus. But they could make sure she was not entitled to free tuition. Amy Bishop had been suspended without pay effective February 12, the day of the shootings. After Lily showed up at Dr. Johnson's class, the university reacted with some urgency. That week a terse letter was fired off to the Bishop house. Anderson could read it to his wife in a jailhouse phone call.

It was one paragraph long and ended with: "Effective February 12, 2010, Dr. Amy Bishop is no longer employed by the University of Alabama at Huntsville." She was fired.

22

Congressman William Delahunt could not hide anymore. He returned to his Quincy home on the South
Shore of Massachusetts to find reporters waiting for
him. It had been ten days since Amy Bishop opened fire
on her colleagues, and the public was hungry for answers. Delahunt insisted his office had no idea that
Amy had engaged in a gunpoint standoff with Braintree
police and refused to drop her weapon despite several
commands that she do so. He said prosecutors didn't
know about the men who had been threatened at Dinger
Ford by Bishop. Delahunt went as far as to claim that the
Braintree police deliberately withheld that information.
The top prosecutor for Delahunt at that time, John Kivlan, also weighed in. Both men were making the rounds,
talking to reporters across Massachusetts to get their
side of the story out.

"All of this outrage that's coming from Braintree
now about how awful it was that she was released—
and believe me, it was wrong—where have these people
been for twenty-three years?" Kivlan said. "Where were
they then? Why didn't Frazier or Solimini or any number
of these officers report that?" He continued, "The issue
really is at this point: Why was Ms. Bishop released
from the police station that night? Who authorized

that? . . . Was there, as Chief Frazier indicated, an intentional cover-up or not? That should really be the focus at this point."

It was the focus of Bill Keating's inquiry. Only the Braintree police were not the only subjects of the renewed investigation. Delahunt was, too. Once the initial reports were completed, it was the responsibility of the state police investigator in the DA's office to follow up on the case. That gave everyone someone else to blame: Trooper Brian Howe. Howe did not show up at the scene that day. Howe did not interview Bishop or anyone in her family until eleven days after the shooting. Howe did not file his report until March of 1987. And that report made no reference to the details of the armed standoff that Bishop had with Braintree Officer Ron Solimini. It did, however, mention that Bishop had been too emotionally distraught to be interviewed. Braintree Lt. Jay Sullivan had seen it differently. He described Bishop as calm and collected in the booking room. Until her mother showed up, that is. Howe had a good reputation on the State Police. He had moved out of state to Savannah, Georgia, but a number of his former brethren reached out to him.

"I did what I was told to do," Howe told a reporter and a State Police union official. "I never got the Braintree police reports. I asked for them over and over again but I never got them. I think we all know why I never got those reports. The Braintree Police Chief did not want me to have those reports." Howe's claim would be bolstered by the newfound evidence. He had indeed repeatedly asked Braintree police for the file, but it was never handed over to him.

Amid all the finger-pointing, there was one thing that everyone could agree upon. Delahunt would say it first. If Bishop had at least been charged she would have had access to psychiatric care. Even the anger management classes recommended after the punch Bishop delivered to the mom's head in the crowded pancake house could have helped. A judge didn't make her do it. "I think an opportunity was missed. I think that was a profound tragedy in this case." *Many* opportunities, was probably a more appropriate way to describe it.

In February, Delahunt hinted that he would not run for reelection. That would be the same month that the *Boston Herald* reported that he blew $560,000 in campaign cash in 2009—much of it on expensive meals and a bloated payroll that included his ex-wife, son-in-law, and daughter. Nickolai Bobrov, who is married to Delahunt's daughter Kara, had raked in $47,732 since landing on the payroll as the congressman's campaign manager in July, including a $10,000 payment that month marked retroactive for "consulting services April–July," the *Herald* found after studying campaign finance records. Delahunt's son-in-law was also listed as treasurer of Delahunt's Campaign for Change political action committee, according to the Center for Responsive Politics. Delahunt's daughter and son-in-law had just purchased a lavish house in tony Milton, Massachusetts, for $620,000. She had plenty of decorating money, thanks to Dad. She pocketed hundreds in campaign cash as a "freelance photographer," records show. Delahunt's political action committee also paid her $421 for photography services in January. Katharina Delahunt, the congressman's ex-wife, pulled in $48,000 as a receptionist and executive assistant for the campaign, a position she's held full-time since 2005, records show. It looked bad. Then again, Delahunt had always had issues dealing with the campaign war chest. There were the vacations at Hedonism and the pricey meals. This was nothing new.

Of course, Delahunt insisted that this talk of retiring

had nothing to do with the allegations that he had mis-handled the Seth Bishop investigation. By then, even Delahunt's friend and fellow Democrat, Massachusetts Governor Deval Patrick, had ordered a review of the state police role in the case, which was not good news for the congressman. "It's critical that we provide as clear an understanding as possible about all aspects of this case and its investigation to ensure that where mistakes were made, they are not repeated in the future," Patrick said in a written statement. That same week, the United States Attorney for the District of Massachusetts, Carmen Ortiz, announced that her office would reopen the 1993 letter bomb case that had named Amy Bishop and her husband, James Anderson, as prime suspects. The Harvard professor targeted with the bomb, Dr. Paul Rosenberg, was ecstatic. "We hope that there is a thorough investigation into this recent crime, so that no one else will be victimized by such senseless violence," Rosenberg said.

Not long after that, Delahunt made it official. He would not run for reelection. The Massachusetts Republican Party, bolstered by the staggering win of Scott Brown in the race for the late Ted Kennedy's senate seat, put up their candidate, Jeff Perry, a former cop from Cape Cod then serving as a state representative. There was also a man ready to run for the Democratic Party: William Keating. The political theater would be riveting. Especially after Keating announced that he had ordered an inquest to hear evidence that Amy Bishop had indeed murdered her brother, Seth in 1986 an that authorities at the time covered up the crime.

23

Bill Keating was in a conference room at his office with state police and prosecutors, poring over the crime scene photographs from what little there was of the Seth Bishop case file. One thing in particular jumped out at him. It was from the shot of Amy Bishop's bedroom. It was a tabloid newspaper sheet. "What's that on the floor?" Keating asked. The trooper had scanned the photos into a computer so they could adjust the viewing angles. Keating zoomed in on what turned out to be a page opened in a copy of the *National Enquirer* from November of 1986. The prosecutors and state police investigators couldn't read the print of the story, just the headline: *"Enquirer World Exclusive—Chilling Details of the Night Patrick Duffy's Folks Died."* It was spread on Amy Bishop's bedroom floor, not far from the spent shotgun shell and the bullet hole in the wall. Keating asked the troopers to track down the story. They did. It was about the shotgun killing of *Dallas* star Patrick Duffy's parents in their bar in Montana, by teenagers who used a truck stolen from a Chevy dealer to flee the scene. The incident was strikingly similar to the crime that Bishop had committed after apparently reading that story in the *National Enquirer*.

The article began: "A blast of frigid night air blew in from Main Street as the bar door swung open around 9:30 p.m. Normal Bailey, the only customer in the place, looked up from his 75-cent beer to see two young, scruffy strangers walk in. The owner, Terry Duffy, smiled from behind the bar and welcomed the pair. That was out of character for Duff, as he was called. Everybody knew he didn't like having shabby strangers, especially young ones, hang around his place, called simply The Lounge.

"But this time Duff made an exception. He didn't chase the guys away—and within minutes it would spell death for him and his wife Babe, who was out back."

The article went on to describe how a customer walked in around 10 p.m. and was greeted by the grisly sight of Patrick Duffy's mother, Babe, dead on the floor. Her husband was slumped over the bar, shot in the chest. A customer had remembered the strangers and reported their descriptions to police. They had been spotted a short distance away—with a semiautomatic 12-gauge shotgun—stealing a pickup truck. The proceeds from the crime, about $90, were found on the suspects, who were arrested after a gunpoint standoff.

Keating did not write the article off as a coincidence. He had already been convinced that the Seth Bishop slaying had warranted a closer look. But the *Enquirer* article spread out on the floor in Amy's bedroom—where the first blast from the Mossberg had been squeezed off—was too much to ignore. He wanted answers and was going to call witnesses to an inquest, much like a grand jury, to get them. He called a press conference at his office in Canton on February 25, 2010.

Keating started out by telling reporters that his investigators had been reviewing the evidence over the two weeks that had elapsed since Amy Bishop had been arrested for the UAH shootings. The fresh look unearthed details that led him to question whether the fatal shooting was in fact accidental.

"Evidence and police records from the shooting appear to be missing," Keating said. "Several inconsistencies have been noted—in original police reports and in interviews." For example, officers who went to the Bishops' 46 Hollis Avenue home after the shooting noted the position of Seth's body alternately as faceup *and* facedown. One report stated that Amy ran out the front door. Another cop wrote that she ran out the back door. The argument Amy Bishop told police she had had with her father the morning of the shooting remained unexplained. There were discrepancies in the reports about whether the shotgun had been fired twice or three times. The Bishops were being uncooperative. Judy Bishop had been an eyewitness to the shooting but her story was incoherent. Two state troopers had knocked at their front door in Ipswich a week earlier. The door was slammed in their face. "An inquest allows witnesses to be subpoenaed," Keating said. "We owe this process to the commonwealth. We also owe this to the grieving families in Alabama."

Keating also let it slip about the *Enquirer* story. He did not mention the publication by name, saying only that the circumstances were similar. But it didn't take long for reporters to figure it out. The murders of Duffy's parents had made headlines across the country the month before the Bishop shooting. It was very strange that not a single Braintree police officer noted the similarities.

"When we were able to retrieve that article and go through it, we were struck with how parallel the circumstances were: shootings with a shotgun, against relatives, and a flight that entailed stealing a car from a car deal-

ership," Keating said. "That could go to the state of
mind of Amy Bishop at the time."

Keating had already sent a letter to Quincy District
Court Judge Mark S. Coven, asking the veteran judge
to lead the inquest. An inquest is rare, especially more
than two decades after a crime had occurred. But Coven agreed to conduct the proceedings, question witnesses under oath, issue subpoenas for documents, and
ultimately issue a report on his findings. A grand jury
would decide whether or not to indict Amy Bishop for
the murder of her brother, Seth.

Every law enforcement official in the state would
weigh in on the Amy Bishop case. There was understandable anger in Alabama that the woman who now
faced capital murder charges for cutting down three of
her colleagues and leaving another three wounded had
such a violent history in the Bay State. Massachusetts
lawmakers and elected officials looked by turns inept,
ridiculous, and corrupt.

Keating was moving into a national political landscape, and he liked it. He wanted to catapult himself
into the hallowed halls of Congress. His name had been
bandied about the minute that Delahunt announced he
was not running again. Those rumors became even more
persistent when in March 2010 Delahunt announced that
he would not seek reelection for the Norfolk County
District Attorney's seat that he had held for a decade.
Before Delahunt dropped from the race, political pundits
had predicted Keating would run for Attorney General
after Martha Coakley easily took over the late U.S. Senator Ted Kennedy's seat. Instead the Democratic Party
was shattered by the upset win of Scott Brown. Now that
Delahunt was out, Keating began to show signs of running for that seat. He planned to move into the district
and began looking for a home in Quincy because the

town had the largest number of registered voters of any of the district's forty-one communities. The last thing Bill Keating wanted was the "soft on crime" taint following him around the campaign trail.

That attitude was clear at the press conference that Thursday afternoon in February. He was a man who was going to take control of the Amy Bishop case and demand real answers. Many viewed it as just for show, a blustery attempt to take charge. It was unlikely that Bishop would stand trial for an old murder in Massachusetts. Not unless the insanity defense her lawyer in Alabama planned to present was unsuccessful. It seemed that her court-appointed attorney, Roy Miller, was going to use all of Amy Bishop's crazy antics as a way to help her avoid a lethal injection; that is unless she preferred electrocution. In that state, death row inmates had a choice. It seems that Bishop's long history of behaving like a lunatic was going to be used to her advantage.

24

Five days after the UAH massacre, Madison County Judge Ruth Hall called Roy Miller. Miller was an attorney in Huntsville, and he had been following the Bishop case closely. News outlets around the country were carrying images of students screaming and crying, the gurneys being raced into awaiting ambulances, cops on scene with their guns drawn, the nutty professor herself. The crime was everywhere.

"Roy," said Hall. "Will you take the Bishop case? A capital murder case?"

Miller hesitated. He knew that his every move would be broadcast out across the country. That said, everyone was entitled to a good defense, and Roy Miller was certain of one thing: He was a good defense attorney. He had been a respected criminal lawyer for forty-one years by then. Still, he prayed before he agreed to take the case, according to the *Huntsville Times*.

"I got with my Lord God and asked Him what I ought to do," Miller said. "He said, 'You want to be a criminal trial attorney, so be it. You got it.'"

His first visit with Amy Bishop came on Wednesday, February 17. He was led into a secure room at the Madison County Jail. Bishop came in wearing the red jumpsuit of a high-security inmate. A prison guard uncuffed her and she sat at a table with her court-appointed lawyer.

"Amy. My name is Roy Miller. I've been assigned to your case," he told her.

"What happened? I don't remember anything. Do I still have a job?" Bishop responded, the lawyer told reporters. Miller was quiet. For a woman who had repeatedly claimed that she had an IQ of 180, she didn't have too much common sense. He didn't know that it had become official yet, but he suspected that it was highly unlikely that Bishop would still be on the UAH payroll. Her husband had also mentioned to Miller that he, too, had an IQ of 180. But that man didn't seem too bright either. For one thing, James Anderson would not stop talking to the media. It was driving Miller crazy.

"I cannot get him to shut up," he would say. "He's a grown man with a full set of teeth. He's a unique individual, and I'll leave it at that."

Miller's first meeting with Bishop at the jailhouse would go on for two hours. When Miller emerged, he shook his head, looked at the reporters assembled outside the facility, and blurted: "Something is wrong with this lady. Her history speaks for itself."

Bishop had told him that she did not remember the shootings at all. She did not remember attending the faculty meeting where the massacre took place. No recollection of stashing the gun, either. She did remember setting up a date night with her husband, though. And while Miller fully admitted, "Hey, I'm an attorney, not a psychologist," he did surmise that his client was a paranoid schizophrenic.

He told the reporters he would have more to say at a press conference Friday morning in the law library near the Madison County Jail. When the time came, he did not disappoint.

"Obviously she was very distraught and concerned over that tenure," Miller said. "It insulted her and slapped her in the face, and it's probably tied in with the Harvard mentality. She brooded and brooded and brooded over it, and then, bingo."

"She gets at issue with people that she doesn't need to and obsesses on it. She just obsesses about the issue," Miller said. "She won't shake it off, even things of no great consequence. She had trouble with friends and foes alike."

Miller had spent time on the phone with the Bishops. Sam was too sick to make the trip and there would instead be a constant flurry of phone calls between the lawyer and Judy Bishop. She was a persistent woman, that Judy Bishop. But Miller did not mind. The conversations helped him garner enough information to ascertain that Amy Bishop "was a whacko." He didn't have any reservations about saying as much either. He called his client a "whacko."

"Good grief," Miller said, "that's the most interesting aspect of this. In my opinion, she's had a serious mental disease for a great number of years. I don't want to get into whether she's been treated or not for that, but I've [tried] a few murders in my life and as I said before I was on the case, I think the case certainly speaks for itself."

He was asked how he would defend her. He laughed a bit. "This is not a whodunit case. What's my defense? Take a damn guess."

25

Amy Bishop would not be seen in a courtroom for more than a month after the massacre. There was no public arraignment on the charges. Instead, Madison County District Attorney Robert Broussard went to the jail on February 15 and recited the charges that had been leveled against her. The closed-door hearing took place in front of an Alabama judge who traveled to the jail for the arraignment rather than have the taxpayers incur the cost of moving Bishop to a courtroom under heavy guard. Before the prosecutor showed up, she called home and spoke to her husband again.

"I only talked to her for two minutes," James Anderson said. "She seems to be doing okay."

Anderson would not be able to visit his wife. He, like everyone else in Alabama, was waiting for the day of her preliminary hearing, which had been scheduled to take place in March. Until then, he was subjected to police coming to his house with search warrants. On March 12, 2010, they showed up again. They seized a video camera and the kids' computers this time. They also took the fat binder that Amy Bishop had compiled about her tenure fight. But there was something else found in the house that made them nervous. They called the bomb squad.

Within minutes, the house at 2103 McDowling Drive was crawling with police officers. Neighbors had been warned to stay inside. Bomb techs used a robot to destroy a piece of PVC pipe that had been found at the home. It was the same kind of PVC pipe that had been used in the letter bomb sent to Dr. Paul Rosenberg back in 1993. Investigators had obtained a copy of the ATF file on the case. No one was going to take any chances with James Anderson. A bomb squad technician examined the remains of the pipe and quickly determined that there were no explosives inside. The commotion was all for naught.

Of course, reporters monitoring police scanners heard the address and rushed to the scene. For weeks, Anderson had been running his mouth. He appeared on *The Today Show. 48 Hours. Dateline NBC*. He told reporters he had gone shooting at a gun club with his wife for target practice three weeks before the murders. He would say, "I knew she had a gun. She wanted to target practice. I don't know why. I went shooting with her a few weeks ago. It was just normal. She was a normal professor with a normal family. It was a normal thing to do."

Now that bomb squad techs were once again poking into James Anderson's house, he didn't have much to say to reporters—especially the reporters who had learned of the 1993 bomb case and asked him about it. "That was nonsense. We were cleared in that case. They had the wrong people, that's all. It wasn't as serious as you all are making it sound. The professor wrote her a good recommendation and everything. We didn't do it."

Then a reporter looked at the police assembled on McDowling Drive. A bomb tech was peeling off his safety suit and putting the robot used to examine the PVC pipe back in a Huntsville PD truck. "Why do you have this kind of pipe in your house?" a reporter asked him. Anderson didn't have much to say this time. "Everything is fine. Frankly, it's none of your business. I have nothing more to say. We just want to be left alone."

26

It was March 23, 2010. Amy Bishop's wrists were cuffed. Her ankles were shackled with a thick chain. Her face bore no expression. She wore the red jumpsuit of a high-security inmate with the words "Madison County Jail" emblazoned on the back. She had white socks and flip-flops. She was flanked by two jail guards and was seated at a table next to her attorney, Roy Miller, and a second criminal defense lawyer who specialized in capital murder cases, Barry Abston. The prosecution would only call one witness, Huntsville Homicide Detective Charles Gray, who attempted to interview Bishop after the shootings. She denied being at the scene of the shootings. Repeatedly. Gray was a veteran officer. He had been with the homicide unit for eight years and with the Huntsville Police Department for twenty-two.

Gray testified that he was listening to his radio as the on-call homicide investigator when he heard a dispatcher announce "a multiple homicide at UA Huntsville on February 12, 2010. Repeat. Multiple homicide at Shelby Center UA Huntsville. All units. All units."

Gray immediately drove to the crime scene. He was told that six people had been shot in the biology department's faculty meeting. Three were dead, and three were taken to Huntsville Hospital. There were six survivors. He pieced together Bishop's day. In the morning she drove her red Cadillac to school. She taught two classes and went home for lunch. She drove her daughter home and asked her husband for a ride back to campus. The Cadillac and her daughter were left at McDowling Drive. When asked about the faculty meeting, Gray said, Bishop claimed she didn't remember being there. Her colleagues, however, remembered every macabre detail, and would share them with Gray upon his arrival.

As the detective testified, Amy Bishop Anderson looked at the floor. Occasionally she would glance up at the cop and focus on what he was saying. Then, without warning, she would slump forward again and stare at her feet.

Gray testified to the facts of the case. The faculty meeting began at 3 p.m. Approximately fifty minutes in, "Bishop Anderson stood up and pointed a handgun at people in the room.

"She shot six people and then left," the detective said. The remaining faculty members barricaded the door, tended to the victims, and called 911, he said. Three people died inside the meeting room.

"The causes of deaths were ruled to be gunshot wounds to the head, and the manner of death was homicide," Gray said. He then named the victims who died: Dr. Adriel Johnson, Dr. G.K. Podila, and Dr. Maria Ragland Davis.

Gray went on to describe the survivors of the shooting. "Two were shot in the head, and one was shot in the chest area, Dr. Luis Cruz-Vera. His wound was almost a head shot, but the bullet appeared to graze his head and go into the chest. Dr. Joseph Leahy and Stephanie Monticciolo were both shot in the head. They are still recovering from their wounds." In fact, both were still hospitalized.

Gray was now assigned to the case full time along with Huntsville homicide detective Kathy Pierce and UAH campus cop James Watkins. Bishop, Gray said, "was in very close proximity to the victims. The three faculty members who were killed sat directly beside her on both sides of the room."

At that point in the testimony, Roy Miller put a comforting hand on his client's arm.

"She seemed calm, she seemed very intelligent," Gray testified. "She said there was no way she was there, no way it happened. 'I wasn't there.' That kept being a reoccurring thing throughout the interview."

Police found the weapon, a 9-millimeter P85 semiautomatic Ruger, in the women's bathroom on the second floor, he testified. It had seven live rounds in its chamber. A black canvas bag that had belonged to Bishop was recovered in the conference room. It had another 15-round magazine.

At that point, Bishop's head snapped up. She stared straight at the homicide investigator. It was as if she was incredulous that police had searched through the trash where she had hidden the gun underneath the blood-stained red plaid jacket she had worn to school. She had that thing stuffed in, wadded under a pile of crunched paper towels.

Gray continued. "She left and made a phone call," he said. "That was later determined to be a call to her husband's cell phone."

The defense attorneys had some questions. Barry Abston would cross-examine the prosecution's witness about where the gun came from. The ATF had tracked the unregistered gun to a store in Troy, New Hampshire.

"Who did the pistol belong to?" Abston asked.

"It was purchased in 1989 by a Donald Proulx in New Hampshire. He bought it specifically for James Anderson," Gray said. This was the same gun that had been tracked to Anderson by the ATF, which had looked at him in connection to the bomb case.

"Do you have any information as to how it came to be in Bishop's possession?"

"I do not," the detective replied.

"In your interview with Anderson did he tell you anything about the pistol?"

"He said he didn't own the pistol." That did not jibe with what Anderson had told reporters. He had repeatedly told the press that the family did have a gun and that his wife had recently gone to a shooting range for target practice.

Abston then suggested that Amy Bishop had asked police after her arrest if she could call the people involved in the shooting. He asked Gray if he remembered that conversation. Bishop's leg fidgeted. She wrung her hands. Her facial expression did not change.

"She asked about them," Gray said, adding that Detective Pierce had conducted much of the interview. "I'd have to review the tape. The interview lasted about two hours."

"Was there anything about Ms. Bishop's behavior that made you think she was on drugs?"

"I don't remember anything specific. We always ask that in every interview."

With that, the defense had no further questions. The prosecution did not call any additional witnesses. They didn't need to. Nine people would tell the same story. Amy Bishop went nuts. She pulled out a gun and methodically shot the colleagues sitting closest to her in the faculty meeting.

The hearing had lasted twenty-five minutes. Judge

Ruth Ann Hall first faced the defense and the prosecution and issued a gag order. No more statements to the press. That went for law enforcement officers, too. The move was made to "ensure the defendant a fair trial." Evidence would be presented to a grand jury in her murder case.

"Any questions?" the judge asked the prosecution and the defense attorneys. No one responded. "There is probable cause to believe the defendant committed the offenses. Bishop Anderson is to remain in custody without bond." In court documents, the defendant was referred to as Bishop Anderson. Investigators called her Bishop.

There would not be a bail package for her to go home to her family while awaiting trial. And her family would not be visiting her in jail. "Too hard for those kids," their grandfather, Jim Anderson Sr., said.

Dr. Amy Bishop was escorted from the courtroom and back to the cell with her bare cot, blanket, and Bible.

27

On May 25, 2010, the judge assigned to undertake an inquest into the death of Seth Bishop completed his review. He had spent three days in closed-door hearings and reviewed piles of evidence. But Quincy District Court Judge Mark Coven was not talking about his findings. Instead, a spokeswoman for the Massachusetts court system, Joan Kenney, issued a statement.

"The report of the inquest into the death of Seth Bishop has been finalized and delivered, according to statute, to the Norfolk Superior Court," she announced. "All documents at the Quincy District Court and the Norfolk Superior Court are impounded by order of the Superior Court."

No one would know what Judge Coven decided. Not for a few days, anyway.

A grand jury was convened in June. A total of twelve witnesses would testify about the Seth Bishop case. It was a two-day process that began on June 9. There were twenty-three jurors impaneled to listen to the testimony. They would even have an opportunity to look at the type of weapon that had cut the eighteen-year-old down. On the first day of testimony, a state trooper, who was assigned to the bomb squad, carried a gun case with a replica Mossberg pump-action shotgun to the courthouse.

It was handed over to a prosecutor. The prosecution wanted to demonstrate how difficult it was to "accidentally" fire a weapon that powerful. A cop would actually show jurors just how much power it took to pull back the trigger of the large shotgun. The prosecution claimed it was ridiculous to suggest the gun could simply "go off" when it had been lying on top of her bed as Amy suggested. It was exactly like the gun that Amy Bishop had "accidentally" fired what was initially believed to be three times on December 6, 1986. Keating's investigators now believe that the evidence did not support the third shot in the ceiling of the kitchen.

A juror present for the testimony said that the grand jury first heard from a prosecutor assigned to Norfolk County District Attorney Bill Keating's office.

"He spent about an hour to give us the backstory," the juror recalled. "It was an unbelievable story. It was amazing that the woman was never really questioned or held."

She would soon learn why. The juror, who asked for anonymity, said every single police officer called to testify—six in all—from the Braintree Police Department requested that they not be present in the courthouse when the former chief, John Polio, gave his testimony.

"It was made clear to us that the other police officers were very intimidated by this chief. They didn't want to even be in the courthouse with him. All of them. It was clear in the testimony. His decision was law. No one questioned him. Even the retired police officers did not want to be in the same room with him," she recalled.

The first witness to testify was Lt. James "Jay" Sullivan, the booking officer. He told the story about the night he was interviewing suspect Amy Bishop and how he had planned to book her on murder charges. He described how Judy Bishop "burst into the room" and told her daughter, "Amy, shut up. Don't say anything."

Sullivan told the grand jury she repeatedly said, "Amy is coming home. Amy is coming home with me."

Startled cops who saw Judy Bishop come into the station with Sgt. Kenneth Brady also testified that they were taken aback when she referred to Chief John Polio by his first name, saying: "I want to see John. Where is John V?" Every Braintree police witness echoed surprise at that.

"They all said the same thing," the juror recalled. "No one called him by his first name."

The cops all testified that Judy was allowed to go into the booking room and take Amy Bishop out a back door. They added that the order came "from the chief."

"You could tell it had been bothering them all these years," the juror said. "They wanted to push this. They wanted to prosecute. The chief said simply, 'no.' That was it. It was crazy to hear about how one guy was able to intimidate so many people."

At the end of the first day, Judy Bishop was called to testify. She was the only eyewitness to the shooting of her son. She was not helpful. Instead, her chest heaved with sobs. Her body began to shake. "At one point it looked like she was going to faint," the juror said. "She was incredibly defensive of Amy. She kept saying, 'Amy didn't do it. It was an accident.'

"Then she would start crying hysterically. She kept saying, 'I'm not well. My husband is not well. I don't know how we can face this.' It was high drama. Very dramatic."

Judy Bishop was asked about the argument Amy had had with her father that day. She denied it happened, claimed she did not remember any sort of "spat," even though it was noted on several police reports.

Tom Pettigrew, the auto mechanic who had been menaced by the shotgun-toting Bishop, testified about how the "crazy bitch" had tried to carjack him. He testified that at first he thought Bishop had a BB gun but the look on her face convinced him that she was much more dangerous than that. He had a message for the grand jurors: "Let's just not forget the people in Alabama, and Seth. This should be more about them than me or anyone else." By then, Pettigrew was living an entirely different type of life. The ATM robbery would catch up with him four years after Amy Bishop attempted to carjack him. He was sentenced to a year in prison and five years' probation after one of his buddies ratted him out. Since then, he had become clean and sober and was working as a chef. He would have to cop to all of that in front of the grand jury. It was critical to prosecutors that the jurors know about the money, and about the words that Amy Bishop had uttered to Pettigrew and his coworker. She did not say, "I accidentally shot my brother to death." She had come up with a cover story about a fictitious husband who had tried to kill her. It was a premeditated story she had to come up with in the minutes after she burst out of her family Victorian and ran through the cold to Dinger Ford.

Another Dinger Ford employee, Jeff Doyle, also testified to the deliberate lie, describing how Amy Bishop had told them to put their hands in the air and that she needed a getaway car because she was "afraid her husband was going to kill her." She repeated that story several times during the gunpoint attack, saying, "I just got in a fight with my husband. I need to get out of here. He's going to kill me," Doyle said. Bishop repeatedly demanded keys to their cars. Of course, Doyle knew nothing about the money that Tom Pettigrew had been counting from the ATM robbery.

There was only one man slated to testify on the second day of grand jury deliberations: Chief John Polio. Polio had been looking forward to his day in court. "I would think from the point of seeing justice done they want to clear the air to determine whether Amy Bishop did accidentally kill her brother or, who knows, the probability that it was more than just an accident," he said when the grand jury proceedings began. "I think it's a good idea I was called to testify."

Polio had told reporters over and over that he had been called to the grand jury on June 10, but the night before, Keating's office called him and told him that his testimony would not be necessary.

In the end, after two days of testimony, the grand jury decided to return a True Bill—which equates to an indictment in the case. "The case was shocking. All the mistakes made. The ineptitude. The power of the chief," the juror said. "We didn't have any other choice."

On June 16, 2010 Amy Bishop was formally charged with the murder of her younger brother Seth Bishop. The indictment read: "Today a Norfolk County grand jury indicted the above-named defendant on a charge of first degree murder." The rest of the case would be impounded by a judge who argued that the materials could be prejudicial when Amy Bishop faces trial in Massachusetts. Grand jury testimony is secret. The inquest was sealed.

Keating was ecstatic with the results. He should have been. Police officers had waited nearly twenty-four years to see Amy Bishop held responsible for her actions on that December day. "In Massachusetts we have evidence that there was a murder," he told reporters gathered at his office in Canton after the indictment was unsealed. Addressing the handling of the old investigation, Keating said, "Jobs were not done. Responsibilities were not met. Justice was not served. The job of a district attorney is to speak for those who can't speak, to seek justice for those who aren't here to demand it."

Polio remained defiant, even after the indictment, spewing: "This doesn't mean anything. She's still innocent until proven guilty."

Keating's office lodged a warrant with Alabama authorities requesting Bishop's extradition to Massachusetts to face the murder charge after her triple-murder case in Huntsville was adjudicated. It might never happen. If Alabama authorities had their way, Bishop would be put to death. Or at the very least spend the rest of her life in an Alabama prison. Still, Keating did not rule out a Massachusetts murder trial, saying: "You never know."

His words would be proven the next day. In a murder case anything can happen—including the defendant trying to take her own life.

28

Amy Bishop insisted that she didn't murder her brother in every interview she had with her attorney, Roy Miller. Right from the beginning she told him, "That was an accident. I swear."

So when a grand jury in Massachusetts ruled Seth Bishop's death an act of cold-blooded, first-degree murder, she took the news hard. Sure, she had been labeled a murderer already. She was facing the death penalty, but seemed not to care much about that. Amy, however, had always worried about what her parents thought of her. And for nearly twenty-four years the Bishop family was really able to convince themselves that Amy had killed Seth accidentally. The indictment was going to make it harder to maintain that delusion. Even as an adult, she started her morning talking to her mother every day. Judy was still in constant contact with James Anderson, bossing him around, telling him what to bring her daughter in jail. Some of her requests were unreasonable, and some were downright ridiculous, Jim Anderson Sr. said. "Things are not good with the Bishops and the Andersons right now," he would say after the murder indictment. Judy Bishop wanted the children sent back to Massachusetts to stay with her in Ipswich. That was not happening, James Anderson told her. Judy wanted him to bring Amy homemade food, which was delusional. Food was not allowed to be brought into a jail facility. Not any kind of food. Judy wanted the kids to call her every day. Judy wanted letters sent more often. "Judy wanted this. Judy wanted that. I truly believe it was Judy Bishop [who] turned Amy into this monster," the elder Anderson said.

Amy Bishop did not become despondent when she was charged with murdering three of her colleagues, critically wounding three others, and trying to kill her friend, Dr. Debra Moriarty. She was not suicidal when she found out she was facing the death penalty. She was suicidal, however, at the idea that her parents would now believe she was not the perfect daughter. The True Bill returned by the grand jury might make her father believe she *did* kill Seth. He hadn't been home that December day in 1986. He may never have read the disparities in the police reports. Samuel Bishop may have taken his wife's word for the events of that day, the events brought on by the shotgun that he had brought into the house. He may have believed that Amy did not intend to hurt her brother. He may not have wanted to know. He may not have known that Amy had refused to drop the weapon when Braintree cops Ron Solimini and Timothy Murphy told her to. The same Solimini whose father Judy had defended at a town meeting just months earlier. He never really thought about why a frightened Amy would have her coat on when she shot Seth, ready to run in the New England winter chill. Sam may never have tried to figure out why there were three blasts fired that awful day: in her bedroom, in their kitchen ceiling, and in Seth's chest. Throughout her adult life, Amy had been doted on. Her mother covered for her. Her father would have wanted to believe both the women in his life. How could he not? The alternative was unimaginable. He would have to live with the possibility that the "spat" he had with Amy before Christmas could have provoked her into such a rage she pulled her winter coat on, practiced firing her father's shotgun in her bedroom, then came downstairs and blew a hole through her brother. He would have to believe she was capable of trying to carjack someone and threatening police at gunpoint. He would have to accept that less patient cops would have been completely justified if they opened fire on his daughter after she ignored repeated demands to drop the shotgun. It was probably much easier to accept his wife's version of events. To believe Amy when she told him "It was an accident, Daddy."

The indictment, however, meant her parents might have to accept that what happened in Braintree on the winter day in 1986 was not an accident. Perhaps that's what Amy thought. The truth was her parents would still vehemently defend her. Sam and Judy Bishop would attack the press and the prosecutors and the police. They would attack the twenty-three jurors who returned the True Bill and got District Attorney Bill Keating the indictment that charged Amy Bishop with murdering her brother. But Amy Bishop had no way of knowing that. Perhaps she thought that she had finally lost her parents' love, the one thing that was most important to her. More important than tenure or James or even her own children. It was the thing that she had been after all along.

Two days after Keating announced that Amy Bishop had been charged with first degree murder, she sat down and wrote a long letter to James. Then she pulled a flimsy razor that the jail issued her for personal grooming across her wrists. It didn't work. She was raced to the hospital, treated for a minor flesh wound, and brought right back to her jail cell. The attempt would not even earn her an overnight reprieve in a cozy hospital bed with sheets.

James Anderson said jail officials never told him his wife had injured herself. Nor would he ever have an opportunity to read the letter she had written him. Jail officials turned the letter over to Huntsville prosecutors. The last time Anderson had seen Amy was on May 9, 2010. They did speak on the phone every Friday night. Most weeks, the focus remained on the kids. She was so concerned about them that on May 9, Mother's Day, he brought the kids for the first time.

"She seemed okay then." James Anderson then sucked in a breath and let out a long sigh. "It's us I worry about."

29

Judy and Sam Bishop were tired of being hounded by the press. It never ended. News trucks outside the house. Phone calls at all hours of the day and night. Judy was devastated. The vow she had made on that awful night in 1986 when she told a Braintree police sergeant, "I just lost one child, I am not going to lose another," was unraveling with each passing day. Seth was dead, and in all likelihood, Amy would be, too, if prosecutors were successful in getting her the death penalty. Just to get the reporters off their backs, Judy and Sam issued a statement that was released to reporters by their attorney, Bryan Stevens. It was written by Sam, the former college professor at Northeastern University, and strongly defended their daughter, Amy. The language was academic, if not a little cold. Sam talked about his wife and daughter as "Judy Bishop" and "Amy Bishop." Throughout the statement Sam and Judy Bishop repeated the refrain that their son's killing was indeed an accident.

"What happened in Huntsville, Alabama was and is a terrible, tragic event. My wife and I feel a deep, unremitting sorrow for the families involved. Lives are irrevocably broken and will never be the same. We understand the pain and the hurt from the loss of a loved family member and we offer our condolences. We cannot explain or even understand what happened in Alabama.

However, we know that what happened 23 years ago to our son, Seth, was an accident. Despite all the finger-pointing among local police, state police, and the District Attorney's Office, there is no evidence that Seth's death was not an accident.

On December 6, 1986, the Braintree Police Department questioned Seth's mother, Judith Bishop, at the house and Amy Bishop (Seth's sister) at the police station the afternoon of the accidental shooting. Their explanation of this accidental shooting has been consistent and has not varied.

The authorities present that day included two Braintree Police Captains, a Lieutenant, and the Chief of Police, and they concluded, after discussions, that the shooting was an accident and that "no charges were going to be brought against Amy Bishop at this time. With current information it would appear to be an accidental shooting. (See the testimonies of Chief of Police John Polio, and Lt. Sullivan; and Lt. Sullivan's Police Report dated December 6, 1986.)

On December 26, 1986, Sam, Judy and Amy Bishop were questioned by Captain Buker, Detective Carey of the Braintree Police, and Brian Howe of the State Police District Attorney's Investigation Unit. They were interviewed separately and a second decision was made by these three individuals that the killing of Seth Bishop was an accident. (See Detective Carey's Report; Brian Howe's Report, "cause of death listed as accidental discharge of a firearm" (dated March 30, 1987); and testimony.)

Mr. and Mrs. Bishop were not involved at all in the investigation except to provide testimony regarding the accident. The facts relating to whether Amy committed a crime occurred prior to the late afternoon of December 6, 1986; and thereafter, any discussions between the various Braintree Police Officers, the District Attorney's Office; and for that matter, the Alabama killings, are irrelevant.

There is absolutely no evidence showing that Amy had any criminal intent to murder someone in 1986. District Attorney Keating's reliance upon a *National Enquirer* article as credible evidence of Amy Bishop's state of mind in 1986 is absurd. The storyline that somehow there was a poor investigation or a cover-up started with the irresponsible and libelous statement of the current Chief of Police, Paul Frazier, who claimed that Mrs. Bishop had removed the investigation file from the police station. Mrs. Bishop was a town meeting member and was not in the position within the town to have any involvement whatsoever with the police department. Mrs. Bishop denies that she ever interfered in any way with the investigation. In fact, it was subsequently discovered that the police department's file had apparently been misfiled or not filed at all for the past twenty years.

The second statement that added to the story that something was wrong with the Town of Braintree's investigation was an irresponsible and false statement of Officer Solimini. His claim that Mrs. Bishop talked directly with Chief Polio is also false and there was no evidence to support such a conversation either on December 6, 1986 or thereafter. Mrs. Bishop, Chief Polio and Chief Polio's secretary all deny that any conversation ever took place.

It is clear that some of the testimonies of the police officers, including Chief Paul Frazier, and Ronald Solimini are motivated by a desire to criticize former Chief John Polio. The Bishops' story is the vehicle and the

Bishop family members are simply pawns in this effort. This is not a case where a family victimized by a crime wishes to have answers and explanations.

We know what happened on December 6, 1986. It is not a case where there was a community outrage of children being shot, drug activity, or a matter that poses any present danger to the public. There is no public outcry to reopen and investigate this case. The story is pressed forward by unrelenting media sensationalism and the talk show hosts' need for something to talk about, and it began with Chief Paul Frazier's irresponsible statements.

The inquest investigation and the Grand Jury have provided no new information of what occurred in the Bishops' house on December 6, 1986. Nothing has changed since the telling of the story in 1986.

The media's coverage of the accident in 1986 has not only been inaccurate in significant respects, but has been sensationalized. It has been painful for us to revisit the events of 1986 at this time as we try to understand the tragic killings in Alabama. We understand that the media event has little to do with us or Seth, or, Amy for that matter. We know that ultimately nothing will happen in Massachusetts and Amy will undoubtedly be spending the rest of her life in Alabama and will not be allowed to return to Massachusetts.

This prejudicial, biased review of the 1986 facts is an enormous waste of public resources that does not in any way provide a benefit to the public and proceeds only for the purposes of assessing blame where no blame was involved, explaining conspiracy theories where there were none, and providing public entertainment. Notwithstanding our horrible memories of December 6, 1986, there were many people who were kind, understanding and caring. We remember, for example, several police officers from the Braintree Police Department coming back in the late afternoon to the house on December 6, 1986 dropping off Chinese food.

We appreciate the kindness of the police officers for weeks thereafter who stopped by just to see how we were doing. We are grateful for the support and the kindness of our neighbors. In 1986, Braintree was a warm, caring community and we continued to live there until 1996. There is an enormous difference between 1986 and today. In 1986 there were no television trucks camped out in front of the house for days, broadcasting the 'news' each night. When in fact, there was no news.

We were grateful for the sound 1986 leadership of Braintree and the District Attorney's Office who had the courage and the intelligence to make responsible decisions.

The death of Seth Bishop was an accident. The 2010 revisiting of the event demonstrates the loss of quality, stability, and civility over the past 24 years. Good judgment has been replaced by sensationalism, conspiracy theories and fear by public officials of making substantive decisions.

The couple's attorney took over from there. Stevens made a passionate argument that "the judicial process followed in reviewing the 1986 events did not comply with fundamental due process rights." He was going to attack the process rather than the people involved. The writing in the statement picked up with his work.

1. The 1986 police reports all consistently, without exception, concluded that the shooting was accidental, but the present Police Chief and the present District Attorney chose to ignore this record.

2. The decision to ignore the 1986 decisions was based on the irresponsible and factually incorrect claim by Chief Paul Frazier that the investigation was not handled properly by his predecessor. Chief Frazier, who was on administrative leave in 1986, was not involved in the 1986 Bishop investigation, and did not testify in the 2010 proceedings.

3. The Bishop family had fully cooperated in the 1986 investigation, but the District Attorney, William Keating, chose to request an Inquest allegedly because they were "not cooperative."

4. The Inquest was properly conducted without media presence. Amy Bishop, who is incarcerated, was understandably not present, and, although cited as the target of the inquest, did not have an attorney representing her interest because there are no provisions in the statutes allowing for an appointment of an attorney to represent her at an inquest.

5. There was testimony by Mr. and Mrs. Bishop and a number of police officers. The Bishops were not allowed to cross-examine or question the prosecution's witnesses and they were not even allowed to offer independent evidence. They were restricted to answering only the questions as posed by the Assistant District Attorney.

6. The report of the Inquest was impounded and was not made available to anyone and yet was the basis for a subsequent convening of the Grand Jury. Interested parties, such as the Bishops, could only speculate as to what the basis was for the Grand Jury proceeding. The Grand Jury process was a repeat of the Inquest with some of the same witnesses, same questions, and same Assistant District Attorney. The Bishops were summonsed to testify, but were again not able to provide any independent statement, and they were not able to

hear other witnesses' testimony, cross-examine or comment on the testimony against Amy. They didn't even know who the witnesses were, much less had access to their testimony to question them or to respond by providing independent statements as to the events in 1986.

7. It is not surprising the Grand Jury voted in favor of an indictment, particularly given the one-sidedness of the presentation. This is in keeping with the common understanding of lawyers that a district attorney is usually able to get a Grand Jury to indict a ham sandwich. The standard of evidence before the Grand Jury is "the preponderance of the evidence," rather than the usual standard in a criminal case of proof beyond a reasonable doubt.

8. And what is most galling and patently unfair was the *Dateline* screening, ONE WEEK BEFORE THE GRAND JURY HEARING. The Braintree Police, the State Police, and the District Attorney—without ever raising the issue of "due process" responsibilities, the judicial standards of "evidence beyond a reasonable doubt", or anything that might provide the balance of fairness that "due process requires"—presented irresponsible speculation, unsubstantiated opinion, and outright factual inaccuracies. They might as well have displayed Amy in prison stripes behind them as they spoke, because they had in effect convicted her on national TV without a trial. The date of the Dateline screening, set well in advance of its screening, would have been communicated to the participants, including the District Attorney who consented to having his press conference included. The one-hour *Dateline* screening, may very well have affected one or more Grand Jurors' judgment and "impaired the presumption of innocence, which is a basic component of a fair trial under our system of criminal justice."

9. There were six important witnesses involved in 1986 events that would have provided critical evidence that are not available 23 years later.

10. In addition, the District Attorney's determination to indict simply means that this decision will be filed in Alabama and Amy will never have an opportunity to realistically and effectively challenge the determination that she is allegedly guilty of murder. Her only choice is to try to get a trial to prove her innocence. All the judicial principles that we talk about and think are important: an opportunity to be heard, a fair trial, the right to challenge the testimony of witnesses, the presumption of innocence, proof beyond a reasonable doubt, prior notice of the charges, and an opportunity to prepare for a hearing, simply did not exist in this case.

The situation in Alabama is very different from the event in Massachusetts in 1986 and the people of Massachusetts should be embarrassed at the government's handling of this matter.

Those that care about justice and fairness should be outraged.

There was a lot of outrage. Only, it was not being leveled at the way prosecutors handled the case in 2010, which is what the Bishops wanted. The outrage instead centered around the way the case had been handled in 1986, when Amy Bishop was not held responsible for murder. Just before she went on to a life of volcanic outbursts, paybacks, alleged assassination attempts, and, finally, a mass murder.

30

By the time Amy Bishop was indicted for her brother's murder, one of her victims, Stephanie Monticciolo, was eating and drinking on her own again. It was significant progress for the biology department assistant who had been shot in the face. Monticciolo had even begun to walk, if only a few steps, with the help of a physical therapist. When Bishop pointed the gun at her, the secretary had turned and covered her face. The bullet actually burst through her right ring finger, family members said, and then hurtled through her brain before it came out her right cheek. A family blog reported that her teeth had been fractured and her sinuses ruined. "This finger saved my life," she told a reporter from the *Huntsville Times*. She held up the crooked ring finger. Her husband, Dominic, told the paper that he had gotten a call from his daughter, Michele, about the shootings on campus as soon as he got home from work. He repeatedly tried to call his wife and got no answer. Then his home phone rang again. The caller ID read *Huntsville Hospital*.

"Is this Dominic?" the hospital administrator asked after introducing herself. "How fast can you get here?"

His wife was in critical condition in the intensive care unit. She would be there for more than two weeks.

Her recovery could take years, and the psychological scars that were inflicted on her by Amy Bishop will never fully heal. But she was grateful for her life and her community. She said as much in an open letter to every student and faculty member at the University of Alabama at Huntsville, her neighbors, family, and friends that was released on the family's blog.

To All The Wonderful Human Beings Who Cared About Me,

I have wanted to write and thank you all for being amazing people. I could never have dreamed of being in contact with so much love and concern.

As my alertness has increased, the knowledge of what blessings you have been to me has overwhelmed me with joy. The prayers that I have received were so kind.

Now that the ability to write you has come to me, I am using this article to say "thank you." My heart is so open with love! I feel more and more blessed to live here, and to work with, go to church with, and be in the same town with, each of you blessed souls. I wish I could send the love and thankfulness that I feel for each of you into words for you to hear.

I thank you for your prayers. I was in such need of them. I have heard that many wrote to other countries to ask for prayers for me, and the blessings I have received are miracles. I am part of a wonderful city and state and country!

Again, thank you so much for your love, prayers and blessings! You are spiritual giants, and I have been so very lucky to have become a part of your prayers and love.

Love, Stephanie Monticciolo

Stephanie's daughter, Michele Monticciolo, believes in good karma, the positive energy that is found in books like *The Secret*. She decided that she was going to turn her family's misfortune into an opportunity to help others. That had always been in her blood. Before her mother was shot, Michele was a life and wellness coach.

In August of 2010, she began delivering inspirational talks across Alabama entitled "On the Other Side: Triumphing Through Any Adversity." She wanted to encourage people who have been through trauma to keep moving. Just like in *The Secret*, she believes that "every negative experience carries the seed for an equally positive one. Perspective is what leans us toward seeing either the negative or positive aspects. Everything is about love and healing through choosing to be aware of what you feel, think, and say."

The family of Dr. Joseph Leahy also set up a blog so that well-wishers could monitor his recovery. When he was transferred from the hospital to a rehab center in April 2010 he could walk for "brief moments." He also choked out a few words for his family. When he was allowed to leave the rehab center in April, he came home to a front yard filled with homemade signs and posters welcoming him back to Pebblebrook Drive. He would be in and out of the hospital for surgeries all summer and into the fall. On September 29, Leahy wrote this on his blog:

> Everyone, I'm going to have another surgery at University of Alabama-Birmingham tomorrow at 10 am or so. They are implanting a titanium plate in my forehead to cover the "dent" in my skull. I'm sure everything will be fine, but please keep me in your prayers. Gin and boys are taking great care of me. Love to all, Joe

The surgery went well. A sister-in-law posted this on the family blog on October 2:

Dear Family and Friends, Joe just called me to say he is back home and doing great! From a picture sent by Ginny via cell phone, the indentation caused by the injury and the subsequent debridement surgery is now smoothed over. He is taking it easy and staying ahead of the pain with meds. He will be going back to UAB on Friday to have the sutures and staples removed. Thanks to all of you for all your prayers. Thanks to Dr. Fisher for doing such a great job. And thank you God for getting Joe through one more surgery.

The tragedy brought the survivors close. Even one of the Huntsville police officers who responded to the carnage kept in touch with the families. Mark Roberts—who had helped emergency workers race Dr. Leahy to an ambulance after the shootings—was married to the woman who became the scientist's occupational therapist. Roberts helped Leahy to the ambulance; his wife would help his slow recovery. The Roberts family had become friends with Joe and his wife and would stop by with homemade lasagna. Leahy's sister-in-law Lisa had another post update on the blog on October 3.

Talked to Joe and Gin. They went to mass tonight, all impressed by Joe's surgery results. They had lasagna brought to them for supper—another one of those stories with all the connections. Mark Roberts brought over the lasagna that he made; he is a Huntsville police officer who was one of the first on the scene at UAH and saw Joe at that time. Mark's wife, Mary, is Joe's occupational therapist, and so it goes. Mark said he could not believe what he saw in Joe.

Thought it would have been a million to one that he might survive.

When Roberts dropped off the lasagna to the professor who he had seen on the floor with a hole blown through the top of his skull, he was amazed. "Truly a miracle," he said. Then he repeated himself. "Truly a miracle."

There was a small blessing for be Leahy that went beyond the fact he survived. The head shot had wiped out any memory he had of the bloodbath that unfolded in the conference room on that February afternoon. His wife, after a doctor's urging, would have to fill him in on the grim details, including the fact that he was shot in the top of the head as he tried to duck under a table. "For some unbelievable reason, Dr. Bishop brought in a gun, stood up, and unprovoked, began to shoot other faculty members in a clockwise fashion," Ginny explained to her husband. Then she recounted how one of his colleagues had pressed napkins to his wound to stop the bleeding and apply pressure to his head. Those actions likely saved his life.

"At least no one died," Joe Leahy responded as his wife talked, according to the *Huntsville Times*.

No, his wife had to tell him, three people did die.

He would tell the *Huntsville Times* about his experience with Amy Bishop, and went as far as saying, "I liked her quite a bit." In fact, he had been one of the people who supported her tenure, just like one of the dead, Dr. Podila.

"That's the toughest part of all," he told the paper. "She was a very nice person. I was one of the faculty who recommended that she be hired. I was supportive of her ever since. I personally liked her quite a bit."

Leahy and Monticciolo stayed in touch with Dr. Cruz-Vera, the other man wounded in Amy Bishop's rampage. He was the least seriously hurt and went back to teaching when the campus opened. At one of the many prayer services held for the victims, he stood up and told mourners about that terrible day. He had been lucky because the bullet that slammed into his chest had hit a chair first, blunting the blow. At first, he didn't even realize that he had been hit. The way he remembered it someone in the meeting began to yell as soon as Bishop whipped out the weapon.

"The only screaming you could hear was, 'Don't do it,'" he recalled at the service. "You cannot have time to know what you're feeling for anyone. You have to see first what is happening." When the bullets stopped, everyone started to care for the wounded, including Cruz-Vera. There were moans and tears and screams.

"I was hearing them. I was trying to comfort them," added Cruz-Vera. Oddly, the sight of his colleagues comforting one another gave him a strange sense of calm. "In that particular moment, I was happy. That was my feeling in that particular moment. When the police came, I was even happier," Cruz-Vera said.

He didn't remember dialing 911, even though he was one of the callers. A 911 dispatcher had heard him say, "I'm going to hand you to someone else. I think I've been hit."

"I was trying to check myself, looking for blood, or some kind of pain. I did not feel anything for like thirty seconds," added Cruz-Vera. "Then I saw the hole. I knew I had been shot." He was raced to the hospital but went home the next day.

The nightmares still grip him at night sometimes. When he talked to the other survivors he found out he was not alone. None of them would ever be fully able to shake the horrific images from their minds. Even Leahy, whose memory of that day was starting to come back in ugly pieces.

31

There had been so many shootings on school properties in the United States that the federal government had to create grants to help the facilities get back on their feet in the aftermath of the violence. The U.S. Department of Education's Office of Safe and Drug-Free Schools were forced to create the Project School Emergency Response to Violence (SERV) fund. The shootings had reached an epidemic proportion. The government was all-too aware of the problem. The media began to compile lists of the deadliest shootings on American soil committed by children and teens.

The list was gruesome and began in 1996 in Moses Lake, Washington. A fourteen-year-old boy named Barry Loukaitis opened fire on his algebra class, killing two students and one teacher. A year later in Pearl, Mississippi, Luke Woodham, a sixteen-year-old student reported to be part of an outcast group, killed two students and his own mother. Months later in West Paducah, Kentucky, fourteen-year-old Michael Carneal fired on students attending a prayer circle. He killed three students and wounded five. Then in 1998 the country was riveted when two youngsters, eleven and thirteen, pulled a fire alarm and then shot other middle school students from nearby woods as the students left the school building. They killed four girls and a teacher, and they wounded ten other students. That same year in Springfield, Oregon, Kip Kinkel, a seventeen-year-old high school student, shot his parents dead and then turned the gun toward his fellow high school students. Two died. Twenty were wounded.

Then came Columbine, an international story of unbelievable brutality. On April 20, 1999 in Littleton, Colorado, eighteen-year-old Eric Harris and seventeen-year-old Dylan Klebold methodically moved through the school, killing twelve people. They also wounded twenty-three others before killing themselves. It didn't end. On January 15, 2002 in New York, New York, an eighteen-year-old student opened fire at Martin Luther King High School in Manhattan and maimed two students. In 2005 at a rural school for Native American students at Red Lake Indian Reservation, Minnesota, a teenager killed nine other students and then himself. Seven people were injured in that rampage.

Colleges and American universities had also been targeted by school shooters. In 1966 at the University of Texas, a student named Charles Whitman pointed a rifle from the observation deck of the University of Texas at Austin's Tower and began shooting in a homicidal rampage that went on for ninety-six minutes. Sixteen people were killed, thirty-one wounded. In 1991, Gang Lu, a twenty-eight-year-old graduate student in physics from China, was upset because he was passed over for an academic honor. He opened fire in two buildings on the University of Iowa campus. Five University of Iowa employees were killed, including four members of the physics department, and two other people were wounded. Lu shot himself after the murders. The most recent attack at a college campus came when a gunman killed thirty-two students in a dorm and in a classroom at Virginia Tech.

Most notably, perhaps, for the University of Alabama victims, was the shooting at Discovery Middle School in Madison, Alabama, a week before Amy Bishop pulled that 9-millimeter from a black satchel and opened fire. A fourteen-year-old was shot in the back of the head. His fifteen-year-old classmate was arrested and charged with murder. The stunned community would learn that Hammad Memon was accused of shooting and killing fourteen-year-old Todd Brown in an execution-style killing. Memon has been ordered to stand trial as an adult for the February 5, 2010 murder. After the shooting, Brown was raced to Huntsville Hospital—the same facility where Bishop's victims would be pronounced dead or treated.

The government responded to the long litany of school shootings by throwing money at the problem. In the fall of 2010, the University of Alabama at Huntsville would receive a federal SERV grant in the amount of $265,000 to "assist in the ongoing recovery efforts." The UAH would commission its own report, hiring an outside firm to compile how well the school had responded in the aftermath of the fatal shootings. The firm was called Witt Associates and it was headed by a former Federal Emergency Management Agency Director named James Lee Witt. They were interested in how UAH communicated to students and faculty while Amy Bishop was still at large, and as far as anyone knew then, armed.

32

Despite the earlier news of her indictment in the 1986 shooting of her brother, Seth, October 2010 brought good news to Amy Bishop's cell. She was officially cleared in the 1993 bomb case. Prosecutors and investigators "engaged in extensive efforts to determine the source of the incendiary device, but despite those efforts, were unable to gather sufficient evidence to bring charges. As a result, the matter was closed," U.S. Attorney Carmen M. Ortiz said in a statement.

"This office does not intend to reopen the matter and we will have no further comment," Ortiz said.

That was it. James Anderson and Amy Bishop were officially cleared in the case. Ted Merritt, the federal prosecutor who declined to press charges against the couple, was still an assistant United States attorney assigned to high-profile federal cases working under the newly appointed Ortiz. Some speculated that it would not do his boss much good to announce that Merritt may have made a mistake when he declined to pursue a grand jury in the case that had been built against James Anderson and Amy Bishop. Ortiz called his review of the bomb case "appropriate and thorough." But Merritt was even more unpopular with police in 2010 than he was in 1993. By then he had successfully prosecuted a Boston Police officer named Harry Byrne who had slapped a Harvard student in the mouth after an arrest. The case was ugly. Byrne was accused of a cover-up. Merritt made his life miserable and in the end Byrne would serve seven years in a federal jail cell—not for the slap, but for the lie that attempted to cover up the assault. Sure, some cops thought Byrne should lose his badge. But his job? There were cop killers in Massachusetts who served less time in prison than Byrne did. Some law enforcement officers had trouble getting along with Merritt. In a strange twist, Byrne was a cousin of ATF Special Agent Bill Murphy, who had always felt that the government should have at least tried to prosecute the Bishops for the bomb sent to Rosenberg. He had worked on the case for years, doggedly pursuing the Bishops from the time the letter bomb was found in 1993 until the case was finally closed in 2001.

The news that the "renewed look at the 1993 bomb case" turned up nothing did not sit well with Murphy, who is now retired. He was still working as a consultant for the ATF because of his expertise with firearms. No one was better at tracing the history of a weapon than he was and the agency was unwilling to lose that expertise when Murphy reached the mandatory retirement age of sixty-five. Murphy remained convinced that the case that he had pursued against Anderson and Bishop from 1993 to 2001 had focused on the right suspects.

"We could tie Jimmy Anderson into the purchase of a roller-lever switch at the South Shore Plaza. And the accounting pad. The same sort of accounting pad that was shipped in the box the bomb was delivered in," Murphy told a colleague at the ATF. "To my dying day

I will say that was very instructive and important. Here is a medical tech guy who has an accountant pad. That's interesting. That's evidence.

"How do you connect Amy Bishop to the case? That's a little harder. How do you connect Bonnie and Clyde? Sure, [Amy] had problems with Dr. Rosenberg, but maybe her husband just wanted to defend the damsel in distress. Anderson? Anderson we had," Murphy told his colleague.

Murphy and others who worked on the Rosenberg case were stunned to hear at Bishop's first court appearance that the murder weapon was a 9-millimeter Ruger, a handgun that had been purchased by a man named Donald Proulx in New Hampshire decades earlier. If the Feds had pursued a case against Bishop and Anderson initially, the gun may have been recovered. Hell, Anderson could have given up its location as part of a plea agreement. Bishop may have voluntarily handed it over to the Feds. Proulx had told agents about the gun back in the 1990s. They questioned Anderson about the weapon, but they could never locate it. Anderson was never charged, so he was not compelled to tell agents where it was hidden.

Murphy never, ever thought that gun would turn up again, certainly not in connection with such a heinous act of violence. Once again, Donald Proulx would be dragged into an investigation for the gun he bought his fellow Eagle Scout, his old pal James Anderson. His name was mentioned by prosecutors in Alabama at Bishop's probable cause hearing. It certainly prompted Bill Murphy to say to his fellow law enforcement officers, "I wonder if those people in Alabama would be alive if we had a chance to find that gun. I guess we'll never know."

It was a question that would likely be asked by prosecutors presenting the case against Amy Bishop in the fall of 2011. Those prosecutors would not work for Norfolk District Attorney Bill Keating. On November 2, 2010, Keating's bid to become a Democratic congressman from Massachusetts was successful. He would replace Bill Delahunt, the longtime congressman who many people blamed, at least partially, for the screw-up in the Amy Bishop case after she killed her brother. The new DA sworn in in January of 2011 was former Massachusetts state Senator Mike Morrissey. Now it would be the burden of all involved to live with the idea that if Amy Bishop had been charged with a single crime in Massachusetts, the bloodshed in Alabama might not have happened at all.

That's the argument raised in some of the lawsuits filed against Amy Bishop and her husband James one year after the UAH massacre. The suits target the school provost as well, arguing that a more thorough background check should have been conducted on Bishop before she was hired. James Anderson is accused of being negligent in allowing his wife to use the gun he had obtained illegally so many years earlier.

In Massachusetts, investigators continued to prepare for a murder trial against Bishop—only former Braintree Police Chief John Polio would no longer be a witness. He passed away of natural causes Christmas week in 2010. His wife was livid at the accusations against her husband and wrote a scathing letter to the editor that was printed in the small newspaper, the *Braintree Forum*, demanding an apology.

Since my dear husband's passing, I have been trying to cope with the grief and anger I feel, as I read each obituary and its references to the Amy Bishop case. It is my contention and belief that Police Chief Paul

Frazier owed my husband an apology for setting in motion a series of events that besmirched John's phenomenal and selfless 37-and-a-half year tenure on the Braintree police force.

Chief Frazier should have said (but he didn't), " 'Please accept my heartfelt apology. I used extremely poor judgment in not calling you on Saturday, Feb. 13, 2010 before speaking with the media regarding the Amy Bishop case.' "

Continuing for another half-dozen paragraphs, the letter laid out in detail the text of, and rationale for, the apology that Mrs. Polio insisted Frazier might have offered her husband (but did not).

But Frazier has yet to issue the apology and it seems unlikely he will be apologizing anytime soon. Many in the Braintree Police Department still feel burned by what happened in 1986 with the Bishop case.

That was a burn that continued to be felt in two states as Amy Bishop sat in a jail cell, awaiting trial on a death penalty case.